DATE DUE

THE ENGLISH COMIC CHARACTERS

THE ENGLISH
COMIC CHARACTERS

by

J. B. PRIESTLEY

. . . We are come
To this great stage of fools . . .

JOHN LANE
THE BODLEY HEAD LTD

First published in 1925
Reprinted 1926
First published in The Week-End Library in 1928

Made and Printed in Great Britain
by T. & A. Constable Ltd., Edinburgh

TO

J. C. SQUIRE

CONTENTS

A 2

THE ENGLISH COMIC CHARACTERS

BULLY BOTTOM

ON any reasonable chronology of Shakespeare's plays, Bottom is the first of his great comic figures. Once we are through the door of Peter Quince's house, when all the company is assembled there, we are at last in the presence of one of the foolish Immortals ; we come to celebrate a staggering feat of parturition, for here, newly created, is a droll as big as a hill. Before this, Shakespeare has shown us through a little gallery of amusing figures, but we have seen no one of the stature of "sweet bully Bottom." In *The Comedy of Errors*, the two Dromios and the rest are nothing but odd curves in a whimsical design. The comedians of *Love's Labour's Lost* are well enough in their way ; the picked and spruce Don Armado, Holofernes with his "golden cadence of poesy," Sir Nathaniel and Moth, all capping one another's fantastic phrases ; but they are little more than quaint shadows that caper for an hour or so on the sunlit lawns of that park in Navarre and then flit out of mind when the sun goes down. In *The Two Gentlemen of Verona*, Speed and Launce (and the dog) are not so much individual creations as lively examples of an admired formula for comic relief, the Elizabethan equivalents of our cross-talk red-nosed gentry. Bottom is neither a curve nor a shadow nor a formula, but a gigantic individual creation, the first of the really great comic figures. " Bottom," writes Dowden, magnificently professorial, " is incomparably a finer efflorescence of the absurd than any preceding character of Shakespeare's invention." And a pity it is that we cannot slip into that comic English Athens and tell Bottom to his large solemn face how fine an efflorescence of the absurd he is, if only because the very extravagance of the phrase would summon back old times to his mind, and before we knew where we were we should find ourselves with tattered play-bills of *Pyramus and Thisbe* in our hands and the whole queer story would be out. The absurd would effloresce before our very eyes.

· Bottom is easily the most substantial figure in the piece. This is not saying a great deal, because *A Midsummer Night's Dream* has all the character of a dream ; its action is ruled by caprice and moonlit madness ; its personages appear to be under the spell of visions or to walk and talk in their sleep ; its background is shadowy and shifting, sometimes breaking into absolute loveliness, purple and dark green and heavy with the night scent of flowers, but always something broken, inconsequent, suddenly glimpsed as the moon's radiance frees itself for a little space from cloud and foliage ; and the whole play, with its frequent talk of visions, dreams, imagination, antique fables and fairy toys, glides past like some lovely hallucination, a masque of strange shadows and voices heard in the night. The characters are on three different levels. There are first the immortals, who have nothing earthy in their composition and are hardly to be distinguished from the quivering leaves and the mist of hyacinths, tiny creatures spun out of cobwebs and moonshine. Then there are the wandering lovers, all poetry and imagination, driven hither and thither by their passionate moods. Lastly there is Bottom (and with him, of course, his companions), who is neither a flickering elf nor a bewildered passionate lover, but a man of this world, comfortably housed in flesh, a personage of some note among the artisans of Athens and, we have no doubt, in spite of certain unmistakable signs of temperament in him, a worthy dependable householder. We suspect that he has, somewhere in the background, a shrewish wife who spends her time alternately seeing through her husband and being taken in by him, for he is essentially one of those large, heavy-faced, somewhat vain and patronising men, not without either humour or imagination, who always induce in women alternating moods of irritation and adoration. Among his fellow artisans, Bottom is clearly the ladies' man, the gallant. He it is who shows himself sensitive to the delicacy of the sex in the matter of the killing and the lion, and we feel that his insistence upon a prologue, "a device to make all well," is only the result of his delicacy and chivalry. Snout and Starveling, who hasten to agree with him, are simply a pair of whimpering poltroons, who have really no stomach for swords and killing and raging melodrama and are afraid of the consequences if they should startle the audience. But Bottom, we feel, has true sensibility and in his own company is the champion of the sex ; he knows that it is a most dreadful thing to bring in the lion, that most fearful wild-fowl, among ladies, and his sketch of the prologue has in it the true note of artful entreaty : "*Ladies, or, Fair Ladies,—I would wish you,—or, I would request you,—or, I would entreat you,—not to fear, not to tremble : my life for yours.*" Such a speech points to both knowledge of the sex and long practice, and given friendly circumstances, the speaker might be a very dangerous man. We should like to see Bottom making love among his own kind ; the result would have startled some of his critics. As it is, we only see him, crowned with an ass's head, suddenly transformed into the paramour of the queen of the fairies, and even in a situation so unexpected, so remote from his previous experience, he acquits himself, as we shall see, very creditably. What would happen if one of the gentlemen who call friend Bottom "gross, stupid, and ignorant," let us say the average professor of English literature, suddenly found himself in the arms of a very beautiful and very amorous fairy, even if his head were not discoverable by immediate sight but only by long acquaintance to be that of an ass ? He would probably acquit himself no better than would Snout or Starveling in similar circumstances, and Shakespeare took care to wave away his Snouts and Starvelings and called the one man to that strange destiny, that "most rare vision," who was worthy of the occasion. Bottom, as Hazlitt said, is a character that has not had justice done him : he is " the most romantic of mechanics."

Against the background of the whole play, which is only so much gossamer and moonlight, the honest weaver appears anything but romantic, a piece of humorous, bewildered flesh, gross, earthy. He is a trades-unionist among butterflies, a ratepayer in Elfland. Seen thus, he is droll precisely because he is a most prosaic soul called to a most romantic destiny. But if we view him first among his own associates, we shall see that he is the only one of them who was fit to be "translated." Puck, who was responsible for the transformation, described him as " the shallowest thickskin of that barren sort," the biggest fool in a company of fools ; but Puck was no judge of character. Bottom, though he may be the biggest fool (and a big fool is no common person), is really the least shallow and thickskinned of his group, in which he shows up as the romantic, the poetical, the imaginative man, who naturally takes command. We admit that he is conceited, but he is, in some measure, an artist, and artists are notoriously conceited. The company of such tailoring and bellows-mending souls would make any man of spirit conceited. Old Quince, who obviously owes his promotion to seniority and to nothing else, is nominally in charge of the revels, but the players have scarcely met together and Quince has scarcely had time to speak a word before it is clear that Bottom, and Bottom alone, is the leader. Quince (" Good Peter Quince," as Bottom, with easy contempt and patronage, calls him) is nothing but a tool in the hands of the masterful weaver, who directs the whole proceedings, the calling of the roll of players, the description of the piece, the casting of the parts, and so forth, step by step. The other members of the company not having a glimmer of imagination, the artist among them, the man of temperament, takes charge. And he alone shows any enthusiasm for the drama itself, for the others are only concerned with pleasing the Duke ; if they do badly, if they should, for example, frighten the ladies, they may be hanged, whereas if they do well, they may receive a little pension.

When Bottom is missing, just before the play is due to begin, and the other players are in despair, their talk plainly shows what it is they have at heart :

SNUG. Masters, the Duke is coming from the temple, and there is two or three lords and ladies more married : if our sport had gone forward, we had all been made men.

FLUTE. O sweet bully Bottom ! Thus hath he lost sixpence a-day during his life ; he could not have 'scaped sixpence a-day : an the Duke had not given him sixpence a-day for playing Pyramus, I 'll be hanged ; he would have deserved it : sixpence a-day in Pyramus, or nothing.

The heart has gone out of the performance, left as it is to these Flutes, Snugs, and Starvelings who can dream of nothing more than sixpence a-day ; but as soon as Bottom, the enthusiast, the romantic, the artist, returns, all is changed, for the leaven of art and imagination begins to work again :

Enter BOTTOM

BOTTOM. Where are these lads ? where are these hearts ?

QUINCE. Bottom !—O most courageous day ! O most happy hour !

BOTTOM. Masters, I am to discourse wonders : but ask me not what ; for, if I tell you, I am no true Athenian. I will tell you everything, right as it fell out.

QUINCE. Let us hear, sweet Bottom.

BOTTOM. Not a word of me. All that I will tell you is, that the Duke hath dined. Get your apparel,

good strings to your beards, new ribbons to your pumps ;
meet presently at the palace ; every man look o'er his
part ; for the short and the long is, our play is preferred.
In any case, let Thisbe have clean linen ; and let not
him that plays the lion pare his nails, for they shall hang
out for the lion's claws.   And, most dear actors, eat no
onions nor garlic, for we are to utter sweet breath ; and
I do not doubt but to hear them say it is a sweet comedy.
No more words : away ! go ; away !

And they and we with them are hustled off to the palace,
heartened and invigorated, ready to agree with Flute and
Quince that bully Bottom has the best wit and the best
person of any handicraft man in Athens.

When the players are first met together and the parts
are being given out, it is not just Bottom's conceit that
makes him want to play every part himself.   Of all
those present, he is the only one who shows any passion
for the drama itself, the art of acting, the enthralling
business of moving and thrilling an audience.   The
others are only concerned with getting through their
several tasks in the easiest and safest manner, with one
eye on the hangman and the other on the exchequer.
But the creative artist is stirring in the soul of Bottom ;
his imagination is catching fire ; so that no sooner is
a part mentioned than he can see himself playing it, and
playing it in such a manner as to lift the audience out of
their seats.   He is set down for the principal part, that

of the lover, but no sooner has he accepted it, seeing himself condoling and moving storms ("That will ask some tears in the true performing of it : if I do it, let the audience look to their eyes ; I will move storms, I will condole in some measure "), than he regrets that he cannot play a tyrant, for he is familiar with Ercles' vein and even shows the company how he would deal with it. Then when Thisbe is mentioned, he sees himself playing her too, speaking in a monstrous little voice. The lion is the next part of any importance, and though it consists of nothing but roaring, Bottom has no doubt that he could make a success of that too, by means of a roar that would do any man's heart good to hear it, or, failing that, if such a full-blooded performance should scare the ladies, a delicately modulated roar that would not shame either a suckling dove or a nightingale. Even when he is finally restricted to one part, that of Pyramus, he alone shows an eagerness to come to grips with the details of the part, particularly in the matter of beards, undertaking as he does " to discharge it in either your straw-colour beard, your orange-tawny beard, your purple-in-grain beard, or your French-crown-colour beard, your perfect yellow." All this shows the eagerness and the soaring imagination of the artist, and if it shows too an unusual vanity, a confidence in one's ability to play any number of parts better than any one else could play them, a confidence so gigantic that it becomes ridiculous, it must be remembered that vanity and a soaring imagination are generally inseparable. It is clear that a man cannot play every part, cannot be lover, tyrant, lady, and lion at once ; but it is equally clear that every man of imagination and spirit ought to want to play every part. It is better to be vain, like Bottom, than to be dead in the spirit, like Snug or Starveling. If it is a weakness to desire to play lover, lady, and lion, it is a weakness of great men, of choice, fiery, and fantastic souls who cannot easily realise or submit to the limitations pressing about our puny mortality. The whole scene, with our friend, flushed and triumphant, the centre of it, is droll, of course, but we really find it droll because we are being allowed to survey it from a height and know that the whole matter is ridiculous and contemptible. These fellows, we can see, should never have left their benches to follow the Muses. But to the gods, the spectacle of Bottom, soaring and magnificent, trying to grasp every part, would be no more ridiculous than the spectacle of Wagner perspiring and gesticulating at Bayreuth : they are both artists, children of vanity and vision, and are both ridiculous and sublime. We can see how droll Bottom is throughout this scene because Shakespeare, having seated us among the gods, has invited us to remark the droll aspects of the situation ; but to

Flute and Starveling Bottom is a man to be admired and wondered at, and probably to Flute's eldest son (that promising young bellows-mender), to whom he has condescended on one or two occasions, our droll weaver is the greatest man in the world, a hero and an artist, in short, a Wagner. We have but to seat ourselves again among the gods to see that " the best in this kind are but shadows," at once droll, heroic, and pitiful, capering for a little space between darkness and darkness.

Once Bottom is metamorphosed, we no longer see him against the background of his fellow artisans but see him firmly set in the lovely moonlit world of the elves and fays, a world so delicate that honey-bags stolen from the bees serve for sweetmeats and the wings of painted butterflies pass for fans, and here among such airy creatures, Bottom, of course, is first glimpsed as something monstrous, gross, earthy. It would be bad enough even if he were there in his own proper person, but he is wearing an ass's head and presents to us the figure of a kind of comic monster. Moreover, he is loved at first sight by the beautiful Titania, who, with the frankness of an immortal, does not scruple to tell him so as soon as her eyes, peering through enchantments, are open. A man may have the best wit and the best person of any handicraftsman in Athens and yet shrink from the wizardries of such a night, being compelled to wear the head of an ass, deserted

by his companions, conjured into fairyland, bewilderingly
promoted into the paramour of the fairy queen and made
the master of such elvish and microscopic attendants as
Peas-blossom and Cobweb and Moth.   But Bottom, as
we have said, rises to the occasion, ass's head and all ;
not only does he not shrink and turn tail, not only does
he accept the situation, he contrives to carry it off with
an air ; he not only rises to the occasion, he improves it.
Now that all the whimsies under the midsummer moon
are let loose and wild imagination has life dancing to its
tune, this is not the time for the Bottom we have already
seen, the imaginative, temperamental man, to come
forward and dominate the scene, or else all hold upon
reality is lost ; that former Bottom must be kept in check,
left to wonder and perhaps to play over to himself the
lover and the lion ; this is the moment for that other,
honest Nick Bottom the weaver, the plain man who is
something of a humorist, good solid flesh among all such
flimsies and whimsies, madness and moonshine.   Does
the newly awakened lovely creature immediately confess
that she is enamoured of him, then he carries it off bravely,
with a mingled touch of wit, philosophy, and masculine
complacency : " Methinks, mistress, you should have
little reason for that : and yet, to say the truth, reason and
love keep little company together now-a-days ; the more
the pity that some honest neighbours will not make them

friends. Nay, I can gleek upon occasion." And we can see the ass's head tilted towards the overhanging branches, as he gives a guffaw at his "gleeking" and takes a strutting turn or two before this astonishing new mistress.

But nothing takes him by surprise in this sudden advancement. His tone is humorous and condescending, that of a solid complacent male among feminine fripperies. When his strange little servitors are introduced to him, the Duke himself could not carry it off better : "I shall desire you of more acquaintance, good Master Cobweb : if I cut my finger, I shall make bold with you"—then turning regally to the next : "Your name, honest gentleman?" Good Master Mustard-seed is commiserated with because "that same cowardly, giant-like ox-beef hath devoured many a gentleman of your House"; all are noticed and dispatched with the appropriate word ; it is like a parody of an official reception. In the next scene, we discover him even more at his ease than before, lolling magnificently, embraced by his lady and surrounded by his devoted attendants, who are being given their various duties. "Monsieur Cobweb, good monsieur"—and indeed there was probably something very Gallic about this Cobweb—"get your weapons in your hand, and kill me a red-hipp'd humble-bee on the top of a thistle ; and, good monsieur, bring me the honey-bag. Do not fret yourself too much in the action, monsieur ; and, good monsieur, have a care the honey-bag break not. I would be loth to have you overflown with a honey-bag, signior." Bottom is clearly making himself at home in Elfland ; he is beginning to display a certain fastidiousness, making delicate choice of a " red-hipp'd humble-bee on the top of a thistle." And if Puck won the first trick with the love philtre and the ass's head, we are not sure that Bottom is not now winning the second, for every time he addresses one of his attendants he is scoring off Elfland and is proving himself a very waggish ass indeed. Even his remarks on the subject of music (" I have a reasonable good ear in music : let us have the tongs and the bones ") and provender (" I could munch your good dry oats. Methinks I have a great desire to a bottle of hay : good hay, sweet hay, hath no fellow ") have to our ears a certain consciously humorous smack, as if the speaker were not quite such an ass as he seems but were enjoying the situation in his own way, carrying the inimitable, if somewhat vulgar, manner of the great Bottom, pride of handicraftsmen, even into the heart of Faerie.

If he shows no surprise, however, and almost contrives to carry off the situation in the grand manner, we must remember that he, like Titania, is only dreaming beneath the moon-coloured honeysuckle and musk roses ; the

enamoured fairy and all her attendant sprites are to him
only phantoms, bright from the playbox of the mind,
there to be huddled away when a sudden puff of wind
or a falling leaf brings the little drama to an end ; and
so he acts as we all act in dreams, who may ourselves be
"translated" nightly by Puck and sent on the wildest
adventures in elfin woods for all we know to the contrary. When Bottom awakes, yawning and stiff in the
long grass, his sense of wonder blossoms gigantically, and
the artist in him, he who would play the tyrant, the lover,
the damsel, and the lion, leaps to life : " I have had a
most rare vision. I have had a dream,—past the wit
of man to say what dream it was : man is but an ass, if
he go about to expound this dream." So fiery and eager
is that wonder and poetry in him which all the long hours
at Athenian looms have not been able to wither away, as
he stands crying in ecstasy in the greenwood, that we
cannot be surprised that his style, which he very rightly
endeavours to heighten for the occasion, should break
down under the stress of it : " The eye of man hath not
heard, the ear of man hath not seen, man's hand is not
able to taste, his tongue to conceive, nor his heart to
report, what my dream was." But no matter ; the
dramatic enthusiast in him now takes command : Peter
Quince (whom we did not suspect of authorship) shall
write a ballad of this dream, to be called Bottom's Dream,

and it shall be sung, by a newly resurrected Pyramus, at the end of the coming play ; and off he goes, his head humming with plans, back to the town to put heart into his lads.   There he plays Pyramus as Pyramus was never played before ; takes charge of the whole company, does not scruple to answer a frivolous remark of the Duke's, and finally speaks the last word we hear from the handicraftsmen.   We learn nothing more of him, but perhaps when the lovers were turning to their beds and the fairies were dancing in the glimmering light, Bottom, masterful, triumphant, was at Peter Quince's with the rest, sitting over a jug or two and setting his fellow players agape with his tale of the rare vision. There was a poet somewhere in this droll weaver and so he came to a poet's destiny, finding himself wearing the head of an ass (as we all must do at such moments), the beloved of an exquisite immortal, the master of Cobwebs and Peas-blossoms, coming to an hour's enchantment while the moon climbs a hand's-breadth up the sky—and then, all "stolen hence," the dream done and the dreamer left to wonder.   Such is the destiny of poets, who are themselves also weavers.

It is a critical commonplace that these Athenian clowns are very English, just as the setting that frames them is exquisitely English ; and it follows very naturally that the greatest of them is the most English.   There is indeed no more insular figure in all Shakespeare's wide gallery than Bottom.   A superficial examination of him will reveal all those traits that unfriendly critics of England and Englishmen have remarked for centuries.   Thus, he is ignorant, conceited, domineering ; he takes himself and his ridiculous concerns seriously and shows no light-ness of touch ; knowing perhaps the least, he yet talks the most, of all his company ; he cannot understand that his strutting figure is the drollest sight under the sky, never for one instant realises that he is nothing but an ignorant buffoon ; the soulless vulgarity of his conduct among the fairies smells rank in the nostrils of men of taste and delicacy of mind ; in short, he is indeed the " shallowest thickskin of that barren sort," lout-in-chief of a company of louts.   But something more than a superficial examina-tion will, as we have partly seen, dispose of much of this criticism, and will lead to the discovery in Bottom of traits that our friendly critics have remarked in us and that we ourselves know to be there.   Bottom is very English in this, that he is something of a puzzle and an apparent contradiction.   We have already marked the poetry and the artist in him, and we have only to stare at him a little longer to be in doubt about certain char-acteristics we took for granted.   Is he entirely our butt or is he for at least part of the time solemnly taking us in and secretly laughing at us ?   Which of us has not

visited some rural tap-room and found there, wedged in
a corner, a large, round-faced, wide-mouthed fellow, the
local oracle ; and, having listened to some of his pro-
nouncements, have laughed in our sleeves at his ignorance,
dogmatism, and conceit ; and yet, after staying a little
longer and staring at the creature's large, solemn face, a
face perilously close to vacuity, have noticed in it certain
momentary twinkles and creases that have suddenly left
us a little dubious about our hasty conclusions ?   And
then it has dawned upon us that the fellow is, in his own
way, which is not ours nor one to which we are accustomed,
a humorist, and that somewhere behind that immobile
and almost vacuous front, he has been enjoying us,
laughing at us, just as we have been enjoying him and
laughing at him.   It is an experience that should make
us pause before we pass judgment upon Bottom, who is
the first cousin of all such queer characters, rich and ripe
personages who are to be found, chiefly in hostelries but
now and then carrying a bag of tools or flourishing a
paint-brush, in almost every corner of this England,
which is itself brimmed with puzzling contradictions, a
strange mixture of the heavy butt and the conscious
humorist.   Bottom is worlds away from the fully conscious humour of a Falstaff, but we cannot have followed
him from Peter Quince's house to the arms of Titania
and seen him in Bank Holiday humour with his Cobwebs

and Mustard-seeds, without noticing that he is something more than a rustic target. He is English, and he is conceited, ignorant, dogmatic, and asinine, but there stirs within him, as there does within his fellow workmen even now, a poet and humorist, waiting for the mid-summer moon. And lastly, he is not dead, he has not left us, for I saw him myself, some years ago, and he had the rank of corporal and was gloriously at ease in a tumble-down estaminet near Amiens, and there he was playing the tyrant, the lover, and the lion all at once, and Sergeant Quince and Privates Snug and Starveling were there with him. They were paying for his beer and I suspect that they were waiting, though obviously waiting in vain, to hear him cry once more : "Enough ; hold or cut bow-strings."

TOUCHSTONE

AS the sunlight filters through the leaves of Arden, scattering gold along its paths and deep into its glades, and the persons of the company there, who " fleet the time carelessly, as they did in the golden age," pass and repass, hardly distinguishable, in their travel-stained russet and green, from the background of forest, we notice that two figures stand out in sharp relief. One is the sad-suited Jaques and the other is Touchstone, bright in his motley. The eye sets these two apart from the rest of the company, and so too does the mind of the spectator, for indeed Jaques and Touchstone stand apart ; they are *in* the forest, but, unlike the others for the moment, they are not *of* the forest ; they remain detached, unconquered by any prevailing enthusiasms, critical. This fact has often been noted by the commentators, and the matter has been put very shortly by Sir Arthur Quiller-Couch : " The comedy, then, is less a comedy of dramatic event than a playful fantastic criticism of life : wherein a courtly society being removed to the greenwood, to picnic there, the Duke Senior can gently moralise on the artificiality he has left at home, and his courtiers—being courtiers still, albeit loyal ones—must ape his humour. But this in turn, being less than sincere, needs salutary mockery : wherefore Shakespeare invents Jaques and Touchstone, critics so skilfully opposed, to supply it." Jaques can be set aside for the moment, left to his endless contemplation : our business is with the critic in motley.

To many it will seem strange that a comic figure should have any claim to the title of critic, whatever that title may happen to mean. But Touchstone is no ordinary comic figure ; he is the representative, and easily the best representative (Falstaff stands by himself), of a special class of comic figures. Unlike most other humorous characters, he has no unconscious absurdities, and that is why he cannot be counted among those who wear the fine flower of the ridiculous ; he is not laughable in himself, he is only droll by vocation. Although he is a Clown, a Fool, he is obviously a superior member of his order ; he is no common buffoon making the most of some natural deformity and finding his fun in bladder play and monkey tricks, but the first of Shakespeare's great Fools, a professional wit and humorist, who publishes his jests and sarcasms daily at the dinner-table instead of bringing them out in octavo in the spring and autumn publishing seasons. Our laughter is his applause.

It may be sometimes necessary for him to turn himself
into a butt, a target for his witty superiors, for, as Celia
remarks, " the dulness of the fool is the whetstone of the
wits " ; but actually there is little of Celia's or anyone's
wit that is whetted on the dullness of Touchstone.
Certainly for us he is no mere butt, for we laugh with
him and not at him.   Even when he is gabbling nonsense,
and that is not often, he is, of course, angling for a laugh
and usually preparing to launch some shrewd home-
truth.   Nor must it be forgotten that the fashion in wit
changes, and that the poor nonsense that Touchstone
occasionally achieves once passed for wit.   When
Elizabeth's dramatists and poets were all scribbling and
the playhouses were packed, language was like a new
glittering toy that had only to be tossed rapidly from
speaker to speaker to set the house in a roar.   Those
were the days when bearded gentlemen, resting between
two epics of endurance and courage, could get drunk on
metaphors and similes and dance with delight under a
shower of puns : language was not yet locked up in
dictionaries but grew apace, new words glimmering on
the horizon like Eldorado.   The verbal battledore and
shuttlecock played by Rosalind, Celia, and Touchstone
in the first act of *As You Like It* may seem a poor game
to us now, but there was a time, before a ball had bounced
at Lord's or Wimbledon, when it was as enthralling as

good cricket or tennis. And even in these scenes there is a taste of the "dull fool's" real quality. The Duke puts the matter in a nutshell when he says of Touchstone : "He uses his folly like a stalking-horse, and, under the presentation of that, he shoots his wit." Indeed, as Jaques surmised, motley is the only wear for a satirist, who will be allowed to utter the most unpleasant truths so long as he jangles his bells. After all, we murmur, as we see the shafts striking home, it is only the Fool : thus our superiority remains unassailed and vanity sits more firmly than ever on its throne.

Jaques too bears witness to the quality of Touchstone. In that famous speech, describing their meeting in the forest, he recognises a fellow philosopher, in his new acquaintance :

> One that hath been a courtier;
> And says, if ladies be but young and fair,
> They have the gift to know 't : and in his brain—
> Which is as dry as the remainder biscuit
> After a voyage,—he hath strange places cramm'd
> With observation, the which he vents
> In mangled forms. . . .

And ever afterwards, he pursues Touchstone through the greenwood as the lovers pursue their ladies, and it is doubtful if some of Touchstone's escapades are not staged purely for his amusement ; though Touchstone,

with the detachment of the genuine humorist, is quite
capable of acting foolishly merely for the satisfaction of
enjoying his own folly.   There is, of course, a strain of
patronage, of easy contempt, in Jaques' attitude towards
Touchstone ; but then rank has not been forgotten even
in Arden, where the courtiers are only playing at
adversity, are only staging a pastoral.   Moreover, this
same strain is discovered in Jaques' attitude towards
everything and everybody.   This cynic-sentimentalist
deserves a word to himself.   Ever since the delighted
commentators have made the discovery that Jaques is
not merely the poet's mouthpiece but a distinct character
like the rest of the personages in the comedy, they have
pressed hard upon him and abused him without stint.
He is almost regarded as the villain of the piece.   One
would suppose that critics are themselves men of thought
rather than men of action, even though they are often
more active than thoughtful, and yet, oddly enough,
the very sight of a contemplative character, such as
Jaques, always sends them into a rage.   From their
diatribes it would be easy to imagine that all the harm
in the world is done by the few eccentric persons who
stand on one side to watch the tragi-comedy of existence
and are content to find entertainment in their own
thoughts.   That the melancholy of Jaques is not a very
serious business, that it is a piece of whimsical self-

indulgence, half play-acting, goes without saying ; but there is room in Arden for his whims just as there is for the antics of the Duke, the courtiers, and the lovers. Though Duke Senior criticises Jaques somewhat roughly, actually there is as much to be said for the one as for the other. Indeed, Jaques is the more consistent, for at the very end, hearing that the usurping Duke has taken to religion, he decides to join him :

> Out of these convertites
> There is much matter to be heard and learned. . . .

Whereas Duke Senior, for all his comfortable talk after lunch, surrounded by his admiring courtiers, of " sermons in stones, and good in everything," shows no great reluctance to return to " the envious court " when his time comes. But though we preach tolerance for Jaques, we need not be blind to his defects. His attitude of mind is sickly. And as he has the apparent softness, so too he has the real hardness of the chronic querulous invalid. Although he can weep over wounded deer, we feel, and rightly too, that there is really something hard, inelastic, griping about his mind. This is because he is that not unfamiliar type, the pure seeker after sensations : he does not identify himself with anything in the whole world, but uses experience as if it were merely a restaurant to dine in ; he can enjoy, for he enjoys his cynicism, his tears, his exquisite disillusion, and not least, for it gives support to all the rest, his massive feeling of superiority, but it is impossible for him to be really happy because never for a single moment can he forget himself. Tasting life is not living any more than dabbling a hand in the water is swimming. Jaques has never waved farewell to pride and secure self-possession and dived into experience, there to discover real sorrow and joy, genuine bitterness, and, perhaps, lasting contentment. He has, like so many of his kind, travelled widely (he boasts of it, you remember, to Rosalind, and is neatly dismissed), but actually he has gained little by it. He imagined, as most of us have done at some time or other, that under the enchantment of distance the one drastic step could be taken, that in some far-off country, among alien faces and to the strange music of foreign tongues, he could somehow slip out of himself, throw off at last the burden of the peering, shivering self, and so do that which he had long affected to despise, namely, grapple with reality, plunge into the wash and roar of real emotions and risk all ; but having imagined this, he found that distance had no magic so potent, and so slipped back into delicate untruth. Love is the enemy of such sentimentalism, whose pallid shoots are scorched by the sun of its joy or beaten down by the hail of its sorrow ; and, it will be noticed, the lovers in the forest,

Orlando, Rosalind, have little time to spare for Jaques,
and dismiss him and his elaborate but flimsy humours
with a shrug. He on his side is clearly uneasy in the
presence of Love and its votaries and is significantly
delighted with Touchstone's mockery of the passion.
After all, what is love but the passionate awareness of
other selves, and what has this—alas !—to do with Jaques
and all his kind ?

Now, as we have seen, Jaques and Touchstone stand
in somewhat similar relation to the rest of the company.
They are " the critics," detached from the main action,
observing, mocking. Whatever departs from sincerity
receives a flick of the whip from them ; or, if you will,
they supply the chorus to the piece ; one, the sad-suited
gentleman, this somewhat eighteenth-century figure with
his exquisite sensibility and his lack of real warm human
sympathy, plays the part of cynical-sentimental-moralistic
chorus ; the other, motleying for more than mere beef
and ale, an embassy from the Spirit of Comedy, supplies
the comic chorus. But while these two seem to run
together most of the way, Touchstone parodying to
Jaques' applause, there is a very real and very important
difference in their respective attitudes. Motley is a
better critic than Melancholy. He is a better critic
because, unlike Jaques, he does not completely detach
himself from his fellow mortals but identifies himself

with them ; he does not say, in effect, "What beasts you are !" but "What fools we are !"; and so, like a true comic genius, he is universal. He does not stand entirely apart, but plays the courtier and the pastoral lover like the rest, only taking care that everything he does shall be plunged into his own atmosphere of exaggeration and absurdity ; he parodies humanity, which looked at from one angle is fundamentally ridiculous, in his own activities and in his own person ; and he does this not simply because he is a Fool, a professional humorist, but also because he is by temperament and inclination a kind of comic philosopher. In this leafy republic of Arden, with its moralising gentlemen, rhyming lovers, passionate shepherds, where so many moods and whims are being dandled throughout the long golden days, the Comic Spirit, scenting profitable negotiations, has established its embassy, and Touchstone, full-dressed in his motley, is the ambassador.

The two persons who know him best and who are responsible for his being in the forest at all, Rosalind and Celia, rather miss his real character : they see the Fool but are blind to the comic philosopher. To them he is "the clownish fool." It is true that Rosalind has her suspicions. When the three of them, wandering in the forest, chance to overhear the passionate Silvius describe the effect of passion, Rosalind exclaims :

Alas, poor shepherd ! searching of thy wound,
I have by hard adventure found mine own.

and Touchstone, very characteristically, makes the whole
thing ridiculous by the use of a few grotesque images :

And I mine. I remember, when I was in love I
broke my sword upon a stone, and bid him take that
for coming a-night to Jane Smile : and I remember the
kissing of her batlet, and the cow's dugs that her pretty
chapp'd hands had milk'd : and I remember the wooing
of a peascod instead of her ; from whom I took two cods,
and, giving her them again, said with weeping tears,
Wear these for my sake. We that are true lovers run
into strange capers ; but as all is mortal in nature, so is
all nature in love mortal in folly.

At which Rosalind remarks :

Thou speak'st wiser than thou art 'ware of ;

and Touchstone replies, enigmatically :

Nay, I shall ne'er be 'ware of mine own wit till I break
my shins against it.

But then two romantic young ladies, grappling with
the problem of lovers and fathers, are no audience for
a humorist of Touchstone's metal. Though both have
wit and humour of their own, one of them, Rosalind,
being famous for her high spirits, much of Touchstone's
humour is of that mysterious and faintly disquieting
kind that they and all their sisters would now describe

as either " silly " or " vulgar."   It has a trick of reducing
everything to one grotesque level ; there is nothing that
it cannot twist into matter for a laugh or, at least, a sardonic
grin ; and against this kind of humour, a very mannish
affair, the feminine mind, which has hallowed chambers
that must be spared the jangle of motley's bells, has always
vigorously protested.   Rosalind's humour—and what
would Arden be without her ripple of laughter !—is very
different from Touchstone's ; it does not try to lay bare
the tangled twisted roots of the Tree of Life, but plays,
like a wavering gleam of sunshine or a cluster of bright
birds, in its high foliage ; it is indeed playfulness, girlish
high spirits, rather than humour, something April-
hearted, for ever dancing on the very edge of tears.
Rosalind, once in the forest and certain of her lover, is
a happy woman who knows that now her greatest ship
is snugly in port she can afford to frolic for an hour at
the quayside.   Secure in her knowledge of their love,
she can torment and tease her bewildered Orlando now
just as afterwards she will continue to torment and tease
him and his children after him.

But if Rosalind and Celia hardly testify to Touchstone's quality as a humorist, they do show us, in one
flash, something of his quality as a man.   They pay
him a magnificent compliment, for they single him out
to be their companion in their flight to Arden.   " Would

he not be a comfort to our travel ? " whispers Rosalind, plotting. Celia replies : " He 'll go along o'er the wide world with me ; leave me alone to woo him." This shows us a new Touchstone. Companions for such a journey are not lightly chosen, even by a Rosalind : our comic philosopher is clearly a man to be depended on ; Motley covers a stout heart. And if Rosalind's suggestion tells us much, Celia's reply tells us even more. " He 'll go along o'er the wide world with me " ; this demure young lady knows her power ; she has the Fool in thrall. He is not then altogether in the service of the Comic Spirit ; his detachment is not complete, for now, it seems, he shows himself to be a romantic at heart, ready to exchange his comfortable berth at court, that dinner-table which is the field of glory for the humorist, for the discomforts and dangers of secret flight. Celia's father, Duke Frederick, may not appear an ideal master for a Touchstone, for he passes from crude villainy to equally crude conversion, and it is not of such unwhole-some persons that a humorist's best audience is composed ; but nevertheless he seems to have held Touchstone (" the roynish clown, at whom so oft your Grace was wont to laugh ") in some esteem, and it says much for the Fool's devotion and courage that he should have quitted such a post to go with the " foolish runaways." When the three of them stagger into the forest, Rosalind crying,

" Well, this is the Forest of Arden," and Touchstone replying, " Ay, now am I in Arden ; the more fool I ; when I was at home, I was in a better place ; but travellers must be content " ; he speaks only the bare truth.   He has flung away safety and comfort and applause for a lady's whim, and has thereby betrayed his genial cynicism. Remove the motley, the cap and the bells, the irreverent jests and sarcasms, the ripe disillusionment, and there remains Touchstone the romantic, set wandering by a glance from his lady's eye, a wave of her hand.   Thus he arrives in Arden.

Romance, however, having enticed him into her own green Arcadia, has to be content with that and nothing more, for once there, Touchstone returns to his ancient loyalties and promptly goes about his own business of parody and mockery, of clowning illuminated by criticism. The chief targets for his wit are the pastoral life, which the Duke and his companions are busy praising with suspicious enthusiasm, and the passion of love, which is leading so many of the gentle foresters into delightful affectations and whimsies.   Touchstone brings scepticism into the greenwood.   Hear him with Corin, the old shepherd :

CORIN. And how like you this shepherd's life, Master Touchstone ?

TOUCHSTONE. Truly, shepherd, in respect of itself,

it is a good life ; but in respect that it is a shepherd's life, it is naught.   In respect that it is solitary, I like it very well ; but in respect that it is private, it is a very vile life.   Now, in respect it is in the fields, it pleaseth me well ; but in respect it is not in the court, it is tedious. As it is a spare life, look you, it fits my humour well ; but as there is no more plenty in it, it goes much against my stomach. . . .

"Zimmermann's celebrated work on Solitude," Hazlitt remarks, "discovers only *half* the sense of this passage." Touchstone does indeed lay a finger, not merely upon the defects of a pastoral life, but upon those human limitations that prevent our declaring, with any sincerity, that any way of life is perfect ; we cannot—more 's the pity !—be in two places at once, cannot have our cake and eat it too ; so every gain enumerated by Touchstone is quickly followed by its corresponding loss, every positive by its negative, and all cancels out.   Well might he conclude by asking, "Hast any philosophy in thee, shepherd ? "   He enjoys himself hugely in the company of this shepherd, to whom he is "Master Touchstone," the gentleman from the court, and not the "dull Fool" or "the roynish clown " ; and it is good to hear him discussing the likeness between shepherds and courtiers, to see him trotting his simple companion from quip to quip, for he does it all with immense relish, and all some-what condescendingly and with a hint of negligence, like a professional conjurer practising a few tricks in front of his landlady. When he concludes by rebuking Corin for playing Pander in Arcadia :

That is another simple sin in you ; to bring the ewes and the rams together, and to offer to get your living by the copulation of cattle ; to be bawd to a bell-wether ; and to betray a she-lamb of a twelve-month to a crooked-pated, old, cuckoldly ram, out of all reasonable match. If thou be'st not damn'd for this, the Devil himself will have no shepherds ; I cannot see else how thou shouldst 'scape,

he appears to be unconsciously parodying the hyper-aesthesia of Jaques, who considered Duke Senior as much a usurper as his brother Frederick because he hunted the deer, the "native burghers" of the place. Most of Touchstone's whimsicalities are of this kind, a distorted reflection of what passes elsewhere in the drama.

When Touchstone does at last meet the Duke, he is at pains to prove that he has been a courtier :

If any man doubt that, let him put me to my purgation. I have trod a measure ; I have flatter'd a lady ; I have been politic with my friend, smooth with mine enemy ; I have undone three tailors ; I have had four quarrels, and like to have fought one.

There is no habitual practice of the courtier's, from dancing to sending shopkeepers into bankruptcy, foreign to him, he tells us ; and then there follows his famous thrust at those elaborate codes of Honour fashionable among gallants of the time. The quarrel that he almost fought was upon the Seventh Cause :

Upon a lie seven times removed ;—bear your body more seeming, Audrey ;—as thus, sir : I did dislike the cut of a certain courtier's beard : he sent me word, if I said his beard was not cut well, he was in the mind it was : this is call'd the Retort Courteous. If I sent him word again, it was not well cut, he would send me word, he cut it to please himself : this is call'd the Quip Modest. If again, it was not well cut, he disabled my judgment : this is call'd the Reply Churlish. If again, it was not well cut, he would answer, I spake not true : this is call'd the Reproof Valiant. If again, it was not well cut, he would say, I lied : this is call'd the Countercheck Quarrelsome : and so to the Lie Circumstantial and the Lie Direct.

JAQUES. And how oft did you say his beard was not well cut ?

TOUCHSTONE. I durst go no further than the Lie Circumstantial, nor he durst not give me the Lie Direct ; and so we measured swords, and parted.

JAQUES. Can you nominate in order now the degrees of the lie ?

TOUCHSTONE. O sir, we quarrel in print, by the book ; as you have books for your good manners : I will name you the degrees. The first, the Retort Courteous ; the second, the Quip Modest ; the third, the Reply Churlish ; the fourth, the Reproof Valiant ; the fifth, the Countercheck Quarrelsome ; the sixth, the Lie with Circumstance ; the seventh, the Lie Direct. All these you may avoid, but the Lie Direct ; and you may avoid that too with an *if*. I knew when seven justices could not

take up a quarrel ; but, when the parties were met themselves, one of them thought but of an *if*, as, *If you said so,
then I said so* ; and they shook hands, and swore brothers.
Your *if* is the only peacemaker ; much virtue in *if*.

All this was very much to the point at the time, for the
book to which Touchstone refers, *Of Honour and Honourable Quarrels* (with chapters on the Lie and its circumstances), had appeared only a few years before the play,
and was probably much in use. Now, the satire passes
us by, for as individuals we have long ago let such nonsense
go whistling down the wind ; but sanity comes first to
individuals and only leavens whole communities after
long ages, and we can still observe empires and republics
occupied with these questions of honour and honourable
quarrels, and their foreign offices giving one another the
Reproof Valiant and the Countercheck Quarrelsome,
and so going forward to the Lie Direct before they set
twenty thousand cannon roaring for honour's sake.
Perhaps the Fool still titters in Arden.

So Touchstone goes wandering about the greenwood,
lounging from one group to another, now mimicking
Orlando's bad verse, now dismissing a yokel, now joining
the tuneful pages in a catch :

> This carol they began that hour,
> With a hey, and a ho, and a hey nonino,
> How that a life was but a flower
> In spring-time, the only pretty ring-time . . .

their voices coming down the years to us and their lovely idle words outlasting so many treatises and grave proclamations ; and so he wanders, fleeting the time between duke and shepherd, courtier and lover. And as it is both his business and his pleasure to mock the fashion of the hour, he does not fail to play the pastoral lover himself. If Orlando must have his Rosalind, Oliver his Celia, Silvius his Phebe, so Touchstone must have his Audrey. For making this somewhat hasty and unequal alliance, he has been taken to task by some of his harsher critics, one of whom claps him forthwith into the dock and proceeds with the charge : " He (Touchstone) does the contrary to Rosalind and Orlando : he misuses this natural life of retirement, in the intention of again casting off Audrey at a convenient season. He uses the opportunity which here presents itself, without possessing the fidelity which according to Lodge's romance should belong to the place. He seems equally devoid of the morality of either town or country." Which shows us how dangerous it is to play the fool in some companies. The fact is that Touchstone cannot worm his way into the idyll ; there is no conventional shepherdess, no lovely pink-and-white and entirely unreal Phebe, for him ; he stays outside the pastoral and remains in this world, and so has to be content with an Audrey, that is, with the kind of damsel really to be found in the countryside, neither superlatively beautiful nor intelligent, but a great gawky country lass. With poor Audrey's unconscious aid, he contrives to stage a most adroit parody of pastoral love as it was depicted by the poets : his sceptical humour lets the east wind of reality into this great artificial palm-house that we call Arden.

He can indite verses as good as, if not better than, those of Orlando, and he certainly has more wit, but—alas !—his lady, being no Rosalind but a genuine creature of the countryside, can understand neither :

When a man's verses cannot be understood, nor a man's good wit seconded with the forward child, understanding, it strikes a man more dead than a great reckoning in a little room.—Truly, I would the gods had made thee poetical.

Audrey, good soul, cannot even pretend to poetry, and has, indeed, a most disarming knowledge of her own limitations, even confessing to a want of beauty, which may be joined in time, in Touchstone's opinion, by other defects, notably sluttishness. None of this, however, disturbs the ironist in motley for an instant : he revels in the incongruity of it all. And while the other lovers, triple-dyed in romance, are swearing eternal constancy, he is calmly welcoming a doubtful ceremony by a doubtful parson because " he is not like to marry me well ; and not being well married, it will be a good excuse for me hereafter to leave my wife." But he is only seeing all round the question. Just as there is a possibility that, after all, the romantic lovers may not be true to one another for ever, so too it is possible that Touchstone may cleave to his Audrey a little longer than a couple of months or so. It is absurd that he should take up with her at all, waving aside, with the most delightful air of condescension, her faithful William ; but then, what would you, surely it is all absurd, this business of courtship and marriage ; rapid mating is in the air and reason has set behind a cloud and Audrey will do as well as another, nay, better than most, because she allows him more scope for his quips ; and for the rest—" As the ox hath his bow, sir, the horse his curb, and the falcon her bells, so man hath his desires ; and as pigeons bill, so wedlock would be nibbling." The relation between Touchstone and his stolid mistress is really nothing but the reverse side, the unpoetical, comic, gross side, of the relation between Orlando and Rosalind, all ardour and bloom and young laughter, beyond the reach of disillusion. Shake them up together and out of them both could be fashioned the actual relations between most men and women in this world ; and Shakespeare, who knew most things, knew this too, and so gave us both sides of the question. By the time he came to create Touchstone, his comic relief had become something more than buffoonery flung in at random, it had become comment, criticism.

That Touchstone's courtship of Audrey, as Hazlitt remarks, " throws a degree of ridicule on the state of wedlock itself," must be admitted, but both his vocation and his natural bent of mind urge Touchstone towards ridicule, and there is, in the last resort, more to be said about his queer courtship than this, more, indeed, than has apparently been said anywhere. That he is not seriously in love is obvious enough, but this is probably only because he cannot be entirely serious about anything. Even his surprisingly romantic devotion to his young mistress Celia, probably has a comical air : we have not heard him on the subject. Yet it is quite possible that a lapse of time that would find Oliver deserting Celia and taking to the forest again, to haunt the neighbourhood of Phebe, now the bored wife of Silvius, would also find Touchstone and Audrey still jogging along together, the gentleman still making mysterious jests and criticisms, and the lady fixing her stolid gaze upon the solid fruits of his jesting and not troubling her head about his whims and fancies. Geniuses, we are told, commonly find their mates among such peasant women, who alone can root them in the earth. For all their Martext and their mock marriage, these two, like the rest of the lovers, come in the end to face Hymen and are duly despatched—

> You and you are sure together,
> As the Winter to foul weather,

—a simile that in such a climate as this suggests a more than common security in their relation. And consider, before we leave him, Touchstone's introduction of his Audrey to the Duke : " A poor virgin, sir, an ill-favour'd thing, sir, but mine own." This, it will be said, is not the speech of a man in love ; nor is it, but it might very well be the speech of a humorist, a dry, sceptical humorist, who is as near to being in love as he is likely to be. "An ill-favour'd thing, sir, but mine own " : the great romantic lovers could never have uttered this ; Rosalind is not Orlando's "ill-favour'd thing " ; and yet the phrase, whose popularity is proved by its frequent misquotation, like a well-shot bolt goes hurtling home and we hear from far-away, faintly but unmistakably, the ringing bell that proclaims the truth of its aim. This world being what it is—and how well Motley knows the world—it describes with more accuracy than all the honeyed, golden speeches of our Romeos and Antonies the actual feelings that men and women, not poets and born lovers, ever ready to shower glittering words upon any newly found deity, but workaday men and women, have for one another ; and as your mood runs, you may throw the emphasis upon "the ill-favour'd thing " and laugh away the follies of youth ; or, more justly, you may wait for the end of the phrase and see the significance, the odd pathos that somehow finds its way into all human relations, of the last three words, " but mine own," and so fall to wondering rather than laughing or perhaps to doing both at once.   And no matter which colouring your mood takes on, you will find some correspondence in colour, some answer, in Touchstone, deep in Arden, for is he not parti-coloured, being in Motley ?   A rare fellow.

THE ILLYRIANS

IF you take ship from the coast of Bohemia—having made your last bow to Perdita and Florizel—and sail for a day in a westerly direction, you will presently arrive at Illyria. There you will find the love-sick melancholy Duke, seated among his musicians, polishing his images and doting upon the " high-fantastical " ; and go but a little way out of the city and you will come upon the stately Countess Olivia among her clipped box-trees, pacing the lawns like some great white peacock, while her steward Malvolio, lean, frowning, and cross-gartered, bends at her elbow. There too, if you are lucky, you may catch a glimpse of the rubious-lipped lovely Viola, stretching her slim legs and swinging her pert page's cloak between the Duke's palace and Olivia's house, delicately breathing blank verse. And if there should come to your ears the sound of drunken catches, and to your nose the smell of burnt sack and pickled herrings, then look for Olivia's uncle, Sir Toby Belch, and his friend, Sir Andrew Aguecheek, and with them, it may be, that dainty rogue, Maria, darting about like some little black and white bird, and Feste the Clown, with his sharp tongue, bright eyes and strange bitter-sweet songs. In and out of doors, there is good company in Illyria, good company whether it is high or low, sober or drunk.

Our present inquiry takes us into the society of the low, the drunken and disreputable company, the comic Illyrians. (It is difficult even to sound the name and remain sober.) Whether Malvolio, who was himself neither drunken nor disreputable but essentially a " grave liver," should have place in the company, is a very debatable question. Most of the comic scenes in the play revolve around him, and it is his antics, his sudden rise and his awful collapse, that form the basis of most of the broader comedy of the piece ; his self-love and swelling vanity, which make him an easy butt for Maria and her grinning troupe, his gravity and pompous airs, are all served up, without mercy, for our entertainment. Yet Malvolio, strictly speaking, is not a comic character. He stands outside the real comic tradition. Although Shakespeare gives some of his speeches a most delicious flavour of absurdity, he does not treat Malvolio as he treats his purely comic figures, whom he regards not merely with a humorous tolerance but with positive delight and relish, encouraging them, as it were, to indulge their every whim. The difference between,

let us say, Malvolio and Sir Andrew Aguecheek is that
Shakespeare handles the one and dandles the other. Sir
Andrew is really a much more contemptible figure than
the serious and capable steward, but then he is so
manifestly ridiculous that he evades criticism altogether,
escapes into a world of his own, where every fresh piece
of absurdity he commits only brings him another round
of laughter and applause. Times change, and we are
more likely to regard Malvolio with some measure of
sympathy than was Shakespeare ; indeed, in spite of his
vanity, to us he is a figure not untouched by pathos, for
the possibility of Olivia falling in love with him (and
she admits his value as an employee) appears to us not
entirely preposterous, nor do his portentous gravity and
puritanical airs seem to us so offensive, now that our
Sir Tobies have been steadily rebuked in the manner of
Malvolio for at least two generations. Sir Toby's famous
reply—" Dost thou think, because thou art virtuous,
there shall be no more cakes and ale "—cuts the ground
from under the feet of a very large number of our energetic
fellow-citizens, whose apparent business it is, Malvolio-
like, to attend to our private affairs and superintend our
morals ; and Sir Toby was fortunate in being able to
make such a rejoinder without being suppressed. Malvolio, we may say, has been steadily coming into his own
for a long time, so that it is difficult for us to regard him

as an unpleasant oddity as Shakespeare did. And perhaps it says something for our charity that, sitting as we are among ever-diminishing supplies of cakes and ale, we can still see something pathetic in this figure.

Shakespeare's sympathies were so wide and his dramatic genius so universal that it is always dangerous to give him a point of view and dower him with various likes and dislikes. Nevertheless it is true to say that certain types of character very clearly aroused his dislike ; and it is also true to say that these are the very types of character that appear to have some fascination for our world. In short, his villains are rapidly becoming our heroes. Thus, Shakespeare clearly detested all hard, unsympathetic, intolerant persons, the over-ambitious and overweening, the climbers and careerists, the " get on or get outs " of this world. When the will and the intellect in all their pride were divorced from tolerance, charity, a love of the good things of this world, they formed the stuff out of which the Shakespearean villains were made. But the Bastard and Iago and Richard the Third are the very characters that some of our modern dramatists would select to adorn three acts of hero-worship. So too, to come down the scale, our friend Malvolio, the pushing puritan, is, under various disguises, the hero of almost one-half of all the American novels that were ever written. Shakespeare, looking steadily at Malvolio with his self-love (" O, you are sick of self-love," cries Olivia to him) and his intolerance, contrives that he shall be covered with ridicule, but never regards him as a comic figure. In spite of his absurdities there are fermenting in him too many of those qualities that Shakespeare detested for him to be a figure of fun. While this conceited and over-ambitious steward struts cross-gartered on the lawn for our entertainment, there flutters across his path, for one fleeting moment, the terrible shadow of that other ambitious underling, Iago. So Malvolio is deceived, abused, locked up and treated as a madman for a short space, and this is his purgation, for Shakespeare saw that his soul was in danger and so appointed for him two angels of deliverance, namely, Maria and Sir Toby Belch.

In the very first speech that Sir Toby makes, when we discover him talking with Maria, he remarks that " care 's an enemy to life," and this we may take to be his philosophy. His time is spent in putting a multitude of things, oceans of burnt sack, mountains of pickled herrings, between himself and the enemy, Care ; and he may be shortly described as a Falstaff without genius, who would have made the fat knight a very able lieutenant. Undoubtedly, he is a very idle and drunken old rip, who forgets his position, which, as the uncle of the Countess, is considerable, his years and his manners, and passes all his time in low company, in the society of his inferiors, either because, like Maria, his niece's chambermaid, they devise entertainment for him, or because, like Sir Andrew, they serve as butts and cat's-paws. But notwithstanding his devotion to sherris sack—and it is doubtful if we ever see him sober—unlike Falstaff Sir Toby does not live altogether in an ideal comic world of ease and merriment ; by much drinking of healths and singing of catches and fool-baiting, and with the assistance of a kind of rough philosophy, a tap-room epicureanism, he certainly tries to live in such a world ; but commonsense and a knowledge of this world's uses keep breaking in from time to time. In spite of his idleness and love of mischief, he is shrewd enough on occasion. Thus, he does not propose to deliver Sir Andrew's ridiculous challenge to the supposed Cesario, because, he declares, " the behaviour of the young gentleman gives him out to be of good capacity and breeding ; his employment between his lord and my niece confirms no less : therefore this letter, being so excellently ignorant, will breed no terror in the youth,—he will find it comes from a clod-pole." He is in no doubt as to the capacity of his admiring dupe, Sir Andrew, who is only encouraged to remain as the suitor of Olivia in order that Toby may amuse himself and mulct the foolish knight of his ducats. His apparently innocent defence of Sir Andrew in the opening dialogue with Maria (" He 's as tall a man as any 's in

Illyria "—and the rest) is, of course, mere impudence, one wag winking at another. Then later, when the confusion between Viola and her brother complicates the action, Sir Toby changes his mind about Cesario, as he has a right to do on the evidence before him, and remarks : " A very dishonest, paltry boy, and more a coward than a hare : his dishonesty appears in leaving his friend here in necessity, and denying him. . . ." And he it is who has the wit to see that the joke against Malvolio has gone far enough—" I would we were well rid of this knavery." Although he vastly enjoys stirring up unnecessary strife and egging on two apparent cowards to fight one another, he shows no reluctance to taking part in any quarrel himself and is certainly no coward. When he himself is hurt, it will be remembered, he makes no complaint (" That 's all one : 'has hurt me, and there 's the end on 't.—Sot, didst see Dick surgeon, sot ? "), and though this stoicism simply covers a fear of being ridiculed, it does argue a stout nature.

Sir Toby, then, is by no means a simpleton. Nor is he, on the other hand, a comic genius like Falstaff, whose world has been transformed into an ideally comic world, whose whole life, whose every speech and action, are devised to further ease, enjoyment, and laughter. Sir Toby, in his own coarse, swashbuckling manner, is witty, but he is not the cause of wit in other men. He does not transform himself into an object of mirth, content so long as men are laughing and the comic spirit is abroad, but, like any bullying wag of the tap-room, looks for a butt in the company. He is really nothing more than an elderly schoolboy with a prodigious thirst and far too much spare time on his hands : the type is not uncommon. Having a more than usual amount of energy, both of brain and body, and no serious powers of application and no sensible objects upon which to expend such energy, his one problem is how to pass the time pleasantly. As he happens to have his existence in a romantic and idyllic world of love and dalliance and fine phrases that offers no employment to a robust and prosaic middle-aged gentleman, and as he, unlike our country squires and retired majors, cannot turn to golf and bridge, there is nothing for it but cakes and ale, the roaring of catches, verbal bouts with the chambermaid and the clown, and mischievous antics played at the expense of such creatures as Malvolio and Sir Andrew Men so situated always seek out low company and are never at ease among their equals. But once among his cronies, Toby enjoys himself with such rollicking abandon that he communicates his enjoyment to us, so that we would not for the world have him different. There is about this drunken, staggering, swaggering, roaring knight, such a ripeness and gusto that his humours are infectious, and

once we are in his riotous company decency and order
seem intrusive and positively ill-natured. He has leave to
keep us out of bed all night, and we would not stint him
of a drop of sack or a single pickled herring. Falstaff
apart, there never was a better bear-leader of a fool.
With what a luxury of enjoyment he draws out and
displays to us the idiocies of the guileless Sir Andrew :

SIR ANDREW. I 'll stay a month longer. I am a
fellow o' the strangest mind i' the world ; I delight in
masques and revels sometimes altogether.
SIR TOBY. Art thou good at these kickshawses,
knight ?
SIR ANDREW. As any man in Illyria, whatsoever he
be, under the degree of my betters ; and yet I will not
compare with a nobleman.
SIR TOBY. What is thy excellence in a galliard, knight ?
SIR ANDREW. Faith, I can cut a caper.
SIR TOBY. And I can cut the mutton to 't.
SIR ANDREW. And I think I have the back-trick
simply as strong as any man in Illyria.
SIR TOBY. Wherefore are these things hid ? wherefore have these gifts a curtain before 'em ? are they
like to take dust, like Mistress Mall's picture ? why
dost thou not go to church in a galliard, and come home
in a coranto ? My very walk should be a jig ; I would
not so much as make water but in a sink-a-pace. What
dost thou mean ? is it a world to hide virtues in ? I did
think, by the excellent constitution of thy leg, it was
form'd under the star of a galliard.
SIR ANDREW. Ay, 'tis strong, and it does indifferent

well in a flame-coloured stock.   Shall we set about some revels ?

Sir Toby. What shall we do else ? were we not born under Taurus ?

Sir Andrew. Taurus ! that 's sides and heart.

Sir Toby. No, sir ; it is legs and thighs.   Let me see thee caper. . . .

Once in his cups, how magnificently he overrides mere precision in speech and commonsense and rises into a poetical kind of nonsense of his own : " To hear by the nose, it is dulcet in contagion.   But shall we make the welkin dance indeed ? shall we rouse the night-owl in a catch that will draw three souls out of one weaver ? shall we do that ? '   With what gusto does he enter into the matter of the duel between Sir Andrew and the disguised Viola, alternately breathing fire into them and then damping it with a report to each one of the other's fury and prowess.   He bustles from one to the other in a very ecstasy of pleasure.   Sir Andrew, he tells Fabian, " if he were open'd, an you find so much blood in his liver as will clog the foot of a flea, I 'll eat the rest of the anatomy "—a remark worthy of Falstaff himself—Sir Andrew is not anxious to fight, but Toby fans his few smouldering embers of courage into a blaze and compels him to send a challenge :

Go, write it in a martial hand ; be curst and brief ; it is no matter how witty, so it be eloquent and full of invention : taunt him with the license of ink : if thou *thou'st* him some thrice, it shall not be amiss ; and as many lies as will lie in thy sheet of paper, although the sheet were big enough for the bed of Ware in England, set 'em down : go, about it. Let there be gall enough in thy ink ; though thou write with a goose-pen, no matter : about it.

Then gives him some further encouragement when the challenge is written :

Go, Sir Andrew ; scout me for him at the corner of the orchard, like a bumbaily : so soon as ever thou see'st him, draw ; and, as thou drawest, swear horrible ; for it comes to pass oft, that a terrible oath, with a swaggering accent sharply twang'd off, gives manhood more approbation than ever proof itself would have earned him. Away !

We can almost hear Toby smacking his lips over the vision of Sir Andrew letting fly a terrible oath, with a swaggering accent sharply twang'd off. Then, with an ever-increasing relish for the situation and with his images swelling at every fresh turn of the farce, Sir Toby confronts Viola with a tale of her incensed opponent awaiting her, " bloody as a hunter," " a devil in private brawl : souls and bodies hath he divorced three ; and his incensement at this moment is so implacable, that satisfaction can be none but by pangs of death and sepulchre : hobnob is his word ; give 't or take 't . . ." —a terrifying picture. Back again he goes to Sir

Andrew, now to damp the knight's faint ardour with an equally terrifying account of his adversary : " Why, man," roars the mischievous old toper, " he 's a very devil ; I have not seen such a firago. I had a pass with him, rapier, scabbard, and all, and he gives me the stuck-in with such a mortal motion, that it is inevitable ; and, on the answer, he pays you as surely as your feet hit the ground they step on. They say he has been fencer to the Sophy." " Pox on 't," cries the startled Sir Andrew, out of his simplicity, " I 'll not meddle with him." But there is no escape for him, even though he should part with his horse as the price of that escape. It is only the unexpected entry of Antonio that robs us of the climax and, possibly, Sir Toby of the horse, but the artful and mischievous knight, who has known something of the satisfaction of those lesser gods who prompt our tyrants and prophets and further our wars and revolutions to pass pleasantly their idle aeons, has had his fun. He has contrived a tale that, with humorous embellishment, will keep any company uproarious between one round of sack and the next, between chorus and chorus.

But if we have enjoyed Sir Toby's antics so much that we have no desire for his immediate amendment, we must leave him with some misgiving, for at the conclusion of the piece we plainly see that those very gods of mischief whom he has emulated in this affair of the duel have now

selected him as the victim of their sport. They who
have allowed him to season his sack with so many herrings
in pickle, have now devised for him a rod in pickle.
This is nothing less than his marriage with Maria, of
which we learn from Fabian's explanation of the joke
against Malvolio at the end of the play. We are told :
" Maria writ the letter at Sir Toby's great importance
(*i.e.* importunity—though this is not strictly true) ; in
recompense whereof he hath married her." Alas !—
poor Toby. We had seen the possibility of such an
alliance throughout the play ; indeed, scene after scene
had shown us Toby edging nearer and nearer to his
doom. We had heard him declare, " She 's a beagle,
true-bred, and one that adores me," in all his fateful
masculine complacency. When the Malvolio jest was
at its intoxicating height, we had heard him shower
compliments on the artful little soubrette, " Excellent
wench " and the rest, had caught him declaring to Sir
Andrew and Fabian, in the ecstasy of his enjoyment,
" I could marry this wench for this device, and ask no
other dowry with her but such another jest." We have
heard him cry to her, " Wilt thou set thy foot o' my
neck ? " and " Shall I play my freedom at tray-trip, and
become thy bond-slave ? " Yet, with the sound of such
dangerous speeches, verbal gun-cotton, still ringing in
our ears, we had thought that the old fox might yet

sniff the air, scent danger and then bolt for freedom. But no, he has walked into the trap. He has been snared, like many another man, not only by a woman but by his own philosophy. " Care 's an enemy to life " he has told himself, and with so much idleness on his hands, with so rich an appreciation of japes and jests, with so great a capacity for mischief and the staging of whims, what could be better than an alliance with Maria, who has proved herself the very queen of humorous strategy, a " most excellent devil of wit," and a most generous purveyor of cakes and ale ? Alas !—had this been any other man's reasoning, he would have seen the folly of it. As it is, he marries, so that the perfect life of comic ease and merriment that he is always attempting to build up may have another prop, and does not realise that he is simply bringing it all down in one awful crash. Who doubts for a moment that what Olivia, with her stately displeasure, could not do, Maria, the erstwhile accomplice and fellow mischief-maker, but now the wife, will accomplish within a very short space ; that Maria the chambermaid, with a comically sympathetic view of sack, catches, and late hours, is one thing, and Maria the wife, with a husband to reform, is another ; that the very wit that could devise such unseemly jests will henceforward be occupied, not in devising others, but in schemes, equally efficacious, for preventing husband Toby

from reaching that large freedom he hitherto enjoyed?
As a last bulwark against care, he has taken Maria to
wife, and now, without a doubt, the old freedom has
vanished and care is about to return in an undreamed-of
measure. Toby's philosophy has undone him, and he
falls; but he falls like a great man. We have caught
his days at their highest point; nevermore shall we see
him, free, spacious, as rich and ripe as a late plum, all
Illyria his tavern, a prince of gusto, good living, and most
admirable fooling; from now on he will dwindle, take
on a cramped and secretive air, and lose his confidence
and zest, for now he will always be discovered, his Maria's
reproaches still shrilling in his ear, a cup too low.

Of one of Sir Toby's boon companions, Feste the
Clown, there is little to be said. Viola, after a bout of
wit with him, sums up the matter admirably:

> This fellow's wise enough to play the Fool;
> And to do that well craves a kind of wit:
> He must observe their mood on whom he jests,
> The quality of persons, and the time;
> Not, like the haggard, check at every feather
> That comes before his eyes. This is a practice
> As full of labour as a wise man's art:
> For folly, that he wisely shows, is fit;
> But wise men's folly, shown, quite taints their wit.

This is an accurate description of Feste's own practice,
for as he lounges in and out of the scene, it will be noticed

that always he plays up to his company. He is a professional entertainer and gives his audiences what he knows will please them. The love-sick Duke feeds upon melancholy, and so to him Feste sings " old and antique " songs and takes delight in his art, but as soon as he has finished the last note of *Come Away, Death*, like the brisk professional he is, he himself shows no trace of melancholy or of any emotion, but is his usual self in a moment, detached, observant, critical, taking his leave with a sly dig at the Duke's melancholy and inconstancy. With the other serious characters, he acts the professional fool but always with a certain reserve and dignity and always with one eye upon the main chance, conjuring another coin into his hand with an ingratiating witticism. Malvolio he really dislikes because the proud and puritanical steward has a contempt for both him and his office (a contempt that Shakespeare himself had probably met with in some Malvolios of his acquaintance), and so he does not scruple to play Malvolio the cruellest trick of all by pretending to be Sir Tobas the parson. With Sir Toby and Maria, Feste appears at his ease and, as it were, with his wit unbuttoned, bandying broad jests with them ; while for the delectation of Sir Andrew, a great admirer of his, he utters the first nonsense that comes into his head. Indeed, in this company of boon companions and midnight caterwaulers, his humour is

all for wild nonsense of a Rabelaisian cast. Such
ridiculous speeches as " I did impeticos thy gratillity ;
for Malvolio's nose is no whipstock ; my lady has a
white hand, and the Myrmidons are no bottle-ale houses "
cast a spell over the rural wits of Sir Andrew, who
pronounces it to be " the best fooling, when all is done."
(There is apparently a lower level of intelligence and
humour than Sir Andrew's ; it is to be found in those
commentators who have pored for hours over these
nonsensical speeches of the Clown's and have then
complained that they could make little of them.)   And
though we may not agree that this " is the best fooling,
when all is done," most of us have regretted that we were
not present at the previous meeting of Sir Toby, Sir
Andrew, and the Clown, when, according to Sir Andrew,
the Clown was in very gracious fooling and spoke of
Pigrogromitus and of the Vapians passing the equinoctial
of Queubus.   Perhaps this is one of the delights that
Heaven has in store for us, or for those of us who are
only fit for a Heaven slightly damaged and humanised.
Wind and rain outside ; indoors a clear fire and a few
tall candles, with sack in plenty ; Sir Toby, straddling
and with nose aglow, on one side ; Sir Andrew gaping
on the other ; and the Clown before us, nodding and
winking through his account of Pigrogromitus and the
Vapians passing the equinoctial of Queubus ; the whole

to be concluded by the catch of *Hold thy peace, thou knave*, with the possibility of being interrupted at any moment by a Malvolio in his nightshirt—here is a hint for the commander of the starry revels.

Sir Andrew Aguecheek is one of Shakespeare's family of simpletons : he is first cousin to Slender and Silence. Life pulses so faintly in this lank-haired, timid, rustic squire that he is within a stride of utter imbecility.   He is really the very opposite of Sir Toby, who is for ever in mischief simply because he has more energy and brains than he knows what to do with, being without any serious purpose, whereas Sir Andrew follows Toby into mischief simply because he is deficient in both energy and brains, and for ever takes the line of least resistance. Without a shred of either self-respect or self-confidence, without volition, courage or sense, he is any man's prey, a toy-balloon blown hither and thither by the slightest breeze.   His social standing and wealth are just sufficient to leave him independent of any occupation or control, a free agent, but being what he is, it means that they are just sufficient to leave him at the mercy of the first rascal he meets.   At first sight, it seems astonishing that a comic character of any dimensions could possibly be created out of such material, and, indeed, only a great genius could have taken these few straws and made of them a creature whose every odd remark and quaint caper is a delight. But it is Sir Andrew's amazing simplicity, his almost pathetic naïvety, his absolute lack of guile, that make him so richly absurd. And with these there goes a certain very characteristic quality, the unanalysable factor, that is present in every remark he makes ; every speech has a certain Aguecheek flavour or smack that is unmistakable ; even as we read we can hear the bleating of his plaintive little voice. His best trait is one that he shares with every simpleton, and that is a childlike capacity for enjoyment, which is really born of a sense of wonder, the ability to marvel at and relish the commonest things, to see the world innocently and freshly, a sense that withers among brighter wits and natures richer in experience but blooms for ever with the extremes of humankind, the utter simpletons and the great geniuses. Sir Andrew has this capacity, and it entitles him to a place at the revels. In spite of his starts and frights, his loss of two thousand ducats and his broken head, it is clear that he has enjoyed himself hugely in the company of his admired Sir Toby, and that he will return to his distant estate bubbling with a confused tale of strange happenings and great personages that will be meat and drink to him for years. It is true that he has been everybody's butt, but then he does not know it ; he is happily protected from all such discoveries and will be all his life ; so that he might almost be said to have the best of the laugh, for whereas the others are living in this world, he is still dwelling in Eden.

There are a thousand things that could be said of this simple creature, for there is probably no better text than a fool, but one particular aspect of him invites our attention. What really tickles us about Sir Andrew, over and above the unanalysable drollery of his speeches, is not what he thinks and feels but the fact that he should not be able to conceal what he thinks and feels. There is somewhere at the back of all our minds a little Sir Andrew Ague-cheek, giggling and gaping, now strutting and now cowering, pluming himself monstrously at one word and being hurled into a fit of depression by the next ; but most of us contrive to keep this little fellow and his antics carefully hidden from sight for the sake of decency and our own self-respect. Some of Sir Andrew's in-genuous remarks have the same effect, or should have the same effect, upon us as the sight of a monkey, which presents us with a parody of human life that is highly diverting but that leaves us somewhat shamefaced : after seeing so many things done openly that we ourselves do in secret, we blush, partly for the monkey that it should make a public show of itself, and partly for ourselves who have so much that is better concealed. The mind of Sir Andrew, such as it is, is as plain to sight as the dial of the parish clock. Almost every remark he makes, innocently revealing, as it does, the ebb and flow of his poor self-esteem, is not only a piece of self-revelation but also a revelation of all our species : this zany, naked to our sight, is uncovering the nakedness of statesmen and philosophers, popes and emperors. How delicious in its candour is his reply to Sir Toby's bantering charge of being " put down " : " Methinks sometimes I have no more wit than a Christian or an ordinary man has : but I am a great eater of beef, and I believe that does harm to my wit." How swiftly following the thought that he may be no better than the ordinary in some particular comes the possible explanation, the eating of beef, to raise the phoenix of his vanity again from its ashes. He remains, at some charge to his purse, with Sir Toby as a suitor to Olivia ; and yet it is clear that the whole idea is Sir Toby's, for Olivia plainly does not favour Sir Andrew, and he knows it, nor does he himself feel any passion for the lady : he has simply allowed himself to be persuaded, caught in the web of Sir Toby's imagination and rhetoric. How swiftly too his vanity plumes itself again at Sir Toby's artful prompting in the matter of his accomplishments ; he can cut a caper, he tells us with a delicious affectation of detachment, and thinks he has the back-trick simply as strong as any man in Illyria.

In the matter of scholarship, which most gentlemen

of his time affected, his simplicity and candour are nothing less than wholesome and refreshing. When Sir Toby declares that " not to be a-bed after midnight is to be up betimes "—and then, plunging into the depths of his learning, brings forth an adage from Lily's grammar— " And *diluculo surgere*, thou know'st— " Sir Andrew provides us with the rare spectacle of a man acting honestly in the face of a classical quotation, by replying : " Nay, by my troth, I know not : but I know, to be up late is to be up late." So too when Sir Toby asks if our life does not consist of the four elements, he replies, indifferently, " Faith, so they say ; but I think it rather consists of eating and drinking "—a notable answer. Again, when the Clown asks whether they will have a love-song or a song of good life, and Sir Toby decides for the former, Sir Andrew speaks for all the novel-readers of our circulating libraries but with more sincerity than they can ever muster when he adds : " Ay, ay : I care not for good life." Most excellent too is his critical observation in reply to the Clown's remark that the knight, Sir Toby, is " in admirable fooling " : " Ay, he does well enough if he be disposed, and so do I too : he does it with a better grace, but I do it more natural." And what could be more revealing than his cry at the indignation meeting after the visit of Malvolio. Maria has said that the steward is sometimes a kind of Puritan.

" O ! " cries Sir Andrew, " if I thought that, I 'd beat him like a dog." When pressed for his exquisite reason, he confesses to having none : indeed, he has no reason at all, but the excitement of the occasion has heated his poor wits and he wishes to make some full-blooded declaration and stand well with the company, like our Sir Andrews who sit in their clubs and tell one another they would " shoot 'em down." How pathetically he echoes Sir Toby. Even when the latter remarks that Maria adores him, Sir Andrew, not to be left out, instantly lights a pitiful rushlight of amatory remembrance : " I was adored once." Yes, he, Sir Andrew, was adored once : it is not true, but for the moment he thinks it is and so contrives to take his place among the swaggering fellows, alongside Sir Toby And perhaps best of all, the very sweet distillation of ingenuousness, is his whisper in the shrubbery when Malvolio, having read the letter, is rehearsing his part as the Countess's husband. As soon as mention is made of " a foolish knight," Sir Andrew is in no doubt as to the person—" That 's me, I warrant you." And when his guess is confirmed by the actual sound of his name, he is almost triumphant— " I knew 'twas I, for many do call me fool," a remark that smacks more of complacency than resignation, as if to be known as a fool did at least single him out for some notice. And how revealing, too, is his conduct

during the duel episode.   He has been told that Olivia
has only shown favour to Cesario in order that her more
backward suitor, the knight, should be encouraged to
accost : he must redeem his credit either by valour or
by policy ; and so he declares for valour, for policy he
hates.   And so he sends a challenge that, notwithstanding his complacent view of its " vinegar and pepper,"
deserves a prominent place in any collection of diplomatic
documents :

Youth, whatsoever thou art, thou art but a scurvy fellow.
Wonder not, nor admire not in thy mind, why I do call thee
so, for I will show thee no reason for 't.   Thou comest to
the Lady Olivia, and in my sight she uses thee kindly : but
thou liest in thy throat ; that is not the matter I challenge
thee for.   I will waylay thee going home ; where if it be
thy chance to kill me, thou kill'st me like a rogue and a villain.
Fare thee well ; and God have mercy upon one of our souls !
He may have mercy upon mine ; but my hope is better, and
so look to thyself.   Thy friend, as thou usest him, and thy
sworn enemy,   ANDREW AGUECHEEK.

Never, in the whole history of the duello, was such good
citizenship exhibited in a challenge.   And when Sir
Andrew learns that his adversary has been fencer to the
Sophy and is a fire-eater, he is swift to declare that he
will not meddle with him, and that had he known that
the fellow had been so valiant and so cunning in fence,
he would have seen him damned before he would have

challenged him. And, of course, Sir Andrew is only talking sense : it would have served the fellow right not to have been challenged. Later, when he has struck Sebastian and has received a pummelling in exchange, he tells Sir Toby to let Sebastian alone : " I 'll go another way to work with him ; I 'll have an action of battery against him, if there be any law in Illyria : though I struck him first, yet it 's no matter for that." No matter at all : he feels, as we all do, that the law is on his side. Our last glimpse of him is somewhat moving, for he has a broken head, received in the company of Sir Toby, who has himself been given " a bloody coxcomb," but nevertheless his admiration and faith are undiminished ; had Sir Toby not been in drink, he tells the company, things would have fallen out very differently ; and at the last, he cries : " I 'll help you, Sir Toby, because we 'll be dressed together." But his idol turns and rends him, calling him an ass-head and a coxcomb and a knave, a thin-faced knave, a gull. These are hard sayings but not too hard for Sir Andrew to swallow, and perhaps they made their peace together afterwards. If not, we can only hope that our simpleton went on his travels and somehow in the end contrived to find his way into Gloucester and into the orchard of Justice Shallow, for there he would find company after his own heart, the great Shallow himself and Silence and Slender, and take his place among such boon companions, seat himself at the pippins and cheese and try to disengage from his tangled mind such confused memories as remained there of Illyria and the roystering Illyrians, his foolish face aglow beneath the unfading apple blossom.

FALSTAFF AND HIS CIRCLE

THE Falstaff of the above title is, of course, the famous fat knight of *Henry IV.*, parts 1 and 2, and has nothing to do with the impostor, the up-river bully, the provincial dupe, of the *Merry Wives of Windsor.* If there is any one who, at this late date, thinks the two are the same, who imagines that our Sir John, companion of Prince Hal, could be successfully gulled by wives of Windsor or any other place, then this essay is not for him : let him read elsewhere, particularly in the works of Maurice Morgann, Hazlitt, and Mr. A. C. Bradley. Our concern, then, is with the two parts of *Henry IV.* and, as a kind of melancholy epilogue, *Henry V.* With the exception of Hamlet, no character in literature has been more discussed than this Falstaff, who is, like Hamlet, a genius, fastening immediately upon the reader's imagination, living richly in his memory, and inviting comment and interpretation that varies with the personality and point of view of every new reader. So splendid is the progress of this great figure in the earlier part of the drama, when he bestrides all Cockaigne

like a colossus, so strange and puzzling is his rejection by
the new king, so melancholy his end, with a heart " fracted
and corroborate," that he engages all our attention and
interest, dwarfing everybody with whom he comes into
contact. For this reason, the comic grotesques who
form his circle and are his foils, Pistol, Bardolph, Hostess
Quickly, Doll Tearsheet, Justice Shallow and his cousin,
Silence, have hardly been noticed, although most of the
comedy in the second part of *Henry IV.* is of their making.
But though we would rather bask in the warmth and light
of this great sun of humour, the fantastic little planets
that revolve about it deserve some attention. We will
leave Sir John in peace for a while, nodding over his
tankard, and creep away to the anteroom where his friends
and followers are assembled.

I

Bardolph, attendant to Sir John and corporal in his
service, is not witty in himself, but he is certainly the
cause that wit is in other men. His face is his fortune,
for at sight of it the comic fancy takes wing. His
famous nose, that everlasting bonfire which Falstaff says
has saved him a thousand marks in links and torches, is
for ever igniting gunpowder trails of comic metaphor.
Such a nose is not cheaply burnished, and Falstaff contends

that the sack Bardolph has drunk would have bought lights as cheap at the dearest chandler's in Europe ; but Bardolph's nose, that salamander consuming the fire of sack, has not been an unprofitable investment. This is proved by the fact that Bardolph has been with his master two and thirty years, after first being hired or " bought " in St. Paul's churchyard, where masterless servants, usually bad ones, were to be had at that time. That he has served his master very faithfully there can be no doubt : it is he who supplies us with one of the most striking tributes to Falstaff's ascendancy over his companions and to his power of winning affection, for after his master's death it is he who cries : " Would I were with him, wheresome'er he is, either in Heaven or in Hell ! "—a genuine cry this, for ever thrown in the blank face of the universe by bereaved humanity. But his real value lies in his nose, warming to life innumerable jests. With such a face near at hand, Falstaff need never be at a loss— though it is only fair to say that there are never any signs that he is at any time at a loss, for his wit gushes out of a perennial spring. It is only right that a comic philo- sopher should be followed by such a gorgeous caricature of a nose. Bardolph is his admiral, bearing the lantern in the poop ; he is the Knight of the Burning Lamp ; Falstaff never sees his face but what he thinks upon hell-fire and Dives that lived in purple ; and he tells the

Hostess, when she says that Bardolph is poor and therefore cannot pay the knight's bill, to "look upon his face; what call you rich? let them coin his nose, let them coin his cheeks." Even the diminutive page finds matter for his newly fledged wit in Bardolph's face. Does he not tell the Prince that Bardolph called to him through a red lattice—"and I could discern no part of his face from the window: at last I spied his eyes; and methought he had made two holes in the alewife's new petticoat, and so peeped through." This is indeed to be, in Gadshill's phrase, "a purple-hued malt-worm." During their long association the number of jokes that Falstaff must have made at the expense of Bardolph's face must be beyond computation; the imagination boggles at the very thought; and we may say that Falstaff has indeed coined his man's nose and cheeks. What could be better, as an example of Falstaffian humour, than his offering Bardolph as security to Master Dombledon for two and twenty yards of satin for a short coat and slops? He would not be without Bardolph for the world, and neither would we. We are sorry he comes to such a bad end.

But if Bardolph is good, his superior officer, Ancient Pistol, is even better. His character is that of the common tavern bully of the period, a fellow who tries to make up for his want of courage and ability by his boldness of

address, a mad moustachio'd, loud-voiced craven, whose
scars are the marks of pots hurled in tavern brawls and
of public beatings. This is a character that brags and
swaggers his way throughout Elizabethan comedy, as
much a formula as the roaring retired Indian Army
major (" By gad, sir ") in modern farce. But Pistol
differs from the other fellows of his class in the fact that
he has a mode of speech all his own. Indeed, he is
actually one of those comic characters that hardly
pretend to real existence at all and are obviously nothing
but grotesque shadows, figures from a comic day-dream.
Pistol's type was common enough, but the Ancient
himself is not of this world. He is a walking parody of
dramatic high-falutin. How many of his speeches are
actual quotations from old plays and ballads we do not
know, and probably never shall know, however the
commentators may busy themselves tracking down his
wild phrases, but it obviously does not matter ; nearly
everything he says sounds like a quotation from some
bombastic drama ; and all of it has a note of its own,
the real Pistol ring. Most of the phrases he uses, strained
and high-flown as they are, would be a trifle ridiculous
even in their context, even though they express overwhelming emotion and refer to matters of great moment,
the massacre of a family or the ruin of great empires, but
brought in as they are by a ragged, drunken rascal to

heighten a tavern quarrel or to silence a rustic, they are ludicrous in the extreme. So much can be said by way of explanation, but no more, for the fact is that it is the actual choice of phrases that matters, the individual flavour of the words, with which only our appreciation of the ridiculous can cope. The comic *idea* in Pistol is very slight and is amply covered by what has been said above ; it is his actual speeches themselves, which we could not possibly invent for him, that make him so funny ; and for this reason there are many admirable persons, lacking the ability to taste, as it were, the absurdity of a phrase, who cannot enjoy Pistol. Thus an intelligent foreigner, who knew his Shakespeare, would perceive that Pistol is a loud-mouthed, swaggering, cowardly bully, of a type familiar in the literature of the time, and leave it at that. He would miss the glorious absurdity, just as many insensitive or over-serious English readers do. For all his passion for quotations, Pistol really has a style of his own, particularly when roused and in Ercles' vein. We can recognise it at once. " Hold hook and line, say I " ; " Have we not Hiren here ? " ; " Die men like dogs ! give crowns like pins ! " ; " What ! we have seen the seven stars " ; " Shall we have incision ? shall we imbrue ? " ; " Base is the slave that pays " ; " Let gallows gape for dog ; let man go free " ; so many of his pithy and weighty phrases leap to the mind that we feel that we could easily compile a Pistol calendar. He is funny enough when he is driven out of the tavern, breathing bad blank verse, but he is even funnier when he bursts into Shallow's orchard with the great news. It is his ability to reach the tragic height on the smallest provocation that makes him so ludicrous. When he tells Falstaff that he is now one of the greatest men in the realm, and Silence, emboldened by his wine, calls attention to goodman Puff of Barson, some dim rural idol of his, what could be more ludicrous than Pistol's tremendous " Puff ! Puff in thy teeth, most recreant coward base ! " or his retort upon a further interruption, this time in song, by Silence ?—

> Shall dunghill curs confront the Helicons ?
> And shall good news be baffled ?
> Then, Pistol, lay thy head in Furies' lap.

Nothing less than blank verse, and blank verse at its wildest, will satisfy Pistol in a moment of excitement. How he raves of " golden times, and happy news of price," of " Africa and golden joys " ; and as he stands there under the apple trees raving, a whole school of drama is being parodied by this ragged grotesque. There is one common type of romantic literature that is summed up to perfection in the single question he addresses to Shallow : " Under which king, Besonian ? speak or die." After the great collapse, Pistol marries Hostess Quickly (and we would give much to hear the phrases he used to assault that battered heart), goes to the French wars, there to steal and run away, and, like Bardolph, comes at last to a bad end. He is not a caricature of something in life, but of something in literature ; his flesh is paper, and his blood ink. He has not been without his influence, for more than once when the tragic dramatist or the high-falutin writer of romances has lost his head, some echo of Pistol has reached us and there has flitted across the scene this grotesque shadow, this strutting parody, out of Shakespeare's comic fancy, and we have been back again in the Boar's Head Tavern or in Shallow's orchard, our tragedy or romance crumpled to nothing, dissolved once more in laughter.

In his somewhat ruthless dispersal and final hunting down of all Falstaff's old associates, so that no shadow should fall on the new and rather easy glory of his hero, Shakespeare was unnecessarily cruel to Dame Quickly, hostess of the Boar's Head Tavern, who is killed off " i' the spital." It may well be, however, that with Falstaff gone, and with him all the old days and roaring nights, she grew careless at the end. Nor can we deny, however friendly we may be towards the dame and her companion, Doll Tearsheet, that both these ladies were in a fair way to encounter that malady to which they succumbed. Nevertheless, the Hostess Quickly of the greater part of *Henry IV.*, though no better than she should be, is at least something better than a ruffianly old trull, and we cannot help feeling that she was deliberately smirched when the blow had to fall upon Falstaff and all his friends. She is the mother of a great line of comic Cockney landladies, charwomen, and the like, in her wandering but vehement speech, her absurd mispronunciations, her oscillation between a native delight in mirth and easy living and an equally innate desire for respectability and a good name in the parish. The type changes very little. Both she and Doll, and particularly Doll, who has forfeited all title to it, are lovers of respectability. Nothing could be truer to nature than Doll's shrill abuse of Pistol, the mere ensign, when his captain is present and willing. The whole scene, with the gross raillery of Falstaff and Doll (and Hostess Quickly's sentimental delight in it—" By my troth, this is the old fashion ; you two never meet but you fall to some discord ") ; the pretended delicacy of the easy dames, with their mutual encouragement, two women among men ; Doll's delight in Falstaff as a man of war ; his lordly " What stuff wilt have a kirtle of "—the secretly delighted male ; the whole scene of broad comedy through which there flickers, as a glance of firelight, a touch of natural unforced sentiment (Doll's " Come, I 'll be friends with thee, Jack : thou art going to the wars ; and whether I shall ever see thee again or no, there is nobody cares " is masterly), is a creation of sheer genius, and lifts Shakespeare as high above his fellows as does any of his great tragic scenes, for they tried in play after play to make such scenes come to life and yet did nothing like this, seemingly thrown out carelessly

But there is not a moment when the Hostess is not alive, not a sentence of her speech that does not ring with truth to nature.   How admirable is her oscillation between anger at Falstaff's debts and continued borrowings and lies and her pride in his patronage and delight in his company.   He has her under a spell, and after abusing her heartily is able not only to escape his present debt to her, but to borrow money from her and then exclaim, with a wave of the hand, " Hostess, I forgive thee : go, make ready breakfast ; love thy husband, look to thy servants, cherish thy guests ; thou shalt find me tractable to any honest reason ; thou see'st I am pacified."   She has all her sex's delight in a plausible and ingratiating rascal, particularly when he bends, like Jove, from a superior social station.   Nothing could better illustrate the characters of both persons concerned than her account of how Falstaff swore to marry her " sitting in my Dolphin-chamber, at the round table, by a sea-coal fire, upon Wednesday in Wheeson week, when the Prince broke thy head for liking his father to a singing-man of Windsor," and how, after goodwife Keech, the butcher's wife, had come in to borrow vinegar for a dish of prawns and Sir John had asked for some prawns, he had told her —delicious flattery—not to be so familiar with such poor people, and had ended by borrowing thirty shillings. One might almost imagine that the dame worked herself up into these rages, excusable as they are, merely in order that Falstaff might cajole her out of them again, as he always does. When she says that she will have to pawn her plate and the tapestry of her dining-chambers to provide him with more money, it is with characteristic impudence that he consoles her by saying that there is nothing like plain glassware and cheap water-colour hangings. And when the poor soul hesitates, the astute old sponger immediately stands upon his dignity and waves the whole matter aside, at which she capitulates and would pawn her very gown that he might have the money. But the "poor soul" slipped into the last sentence without permission and has no right to be there, for though she was scandalously plucked, she received as much as she gave ; she had the company of the famous Sir John Falstaff, and though it is an excellent thing to have one's bills paid, to keep one's plate and tapestries from the pawnshop, to be accounted respectable and stand well with Master Tisick, the deputy, and Master

Dumb, the minister, it is even better to have the company, in his hours of glorious ease, of Sir John Falstaff. That this is not merely our opinion, born of hero-worship and a safe distance that keeps plate and tapestry intact, but her opinion too, is proved by her own testimony : " Well, fare thee well : I have known thee these twenty-nine years, come peascod time ; but an honester and truer-hearted man,—well, fare thee well." Falstaff is neither honest nor true-hearted, as she has known to her cost, but he has her admiration and affection, and so she uses the words of praise that come most easily to her tongue. It is she, of course, who rings down the curtain upon this companion of princes, this erstwhile emperor of Cockaigne, in a speech that is famous, and well deserves to be, for it has all the tragi-comedy of this life blended together, with exquisite art, in its seemingly natural artless progress : " 'A made a fine end, and went away, an it had been any christom child : 'a parted even just between twelve and one, even at the turning o' the tide : for after I saw him fumble with the sheets, and play with flowers, and smile upon his fingers' ends, I knew there was but one way ; for his nose was as sharp as a pen, and 'a babbled of green fields."

All these figures about Falstaff, comic as they are in themselves, chiefly serve as foils to him ; they are the grotesque landscape lit up by the summer lightning of his wit and humour. Not one is a better foil than Justice Shallow. Except in years, he is everything that Falstaff is not. When they made Sir John, the gods dipped their hands deep in the stuff of creation, so that he overflows with everything that a man could have, short of virtue ; he is a liberal helping of humanity ; immense in body, "larding the lean earth" as he goes his way upon it ; brimmed with energy, in spite of his years and bulk ; crammed with experience and master of almost every occasion that comes his way ; overflowing with wit and humour ; bursting with good spirits and laughter ; he is an alderman's feast of a man. Shallow, his contemporary, is the shadow of a lenten breakfast, who, even in his youth, was "like a man made after supper of a cheese-paring," a forked radish, with a head fantastically carved upon it with a knife, and now that his wisp of a carcase and his wisp of a mind have entered into their winter, there is hardly anything left of him but a few bones, a mouthful of silly phrases, and an idea or two, kept together only by his notion of his own importance. He has little to say, being as feeble in mind as in body, but being the greatest man in the district, and feeling that he ought to be saying something all the time, he repeats himself over and over again, without paying much attention to the person to whom he is talking, in a manner peculiar to half-witted self-important old men. This fussy empty mode of speech has never been caught so well as it is in Shallow : " Come on, come on, come on, sir ; give me your hand, sir ; give me your hand, sir ; an early stirrer, by the Rood." These accents may be overheard any day in the smoking room of almost any club. After hearing Shallow talk, Falstaff, the clear-sighted old rascal, exclaims : " Lord, Lord, how subject we old men are to this vice of lying." That wild youth of his, to which Shallow so often refers, to the admiration of Silence, is entirely imaginary ; Falstaff remembers him and tells us how " 'a came ever in the rearward of the fashion ; and sung those tunes to the overscutch'd huswives that he heard the carmen whistle, and sware they were his Fancies or his Good-nights," and you could have thrust him and all his apparel into an eel-skin, the case of a treble hautboy was a mansion to him. We can see him, pinched and rural and for ever behind the fashion, palely trembling on the edge of debauchery. And now fifty years have ripened these shadowy adventures into a kind of reality, and as he drags his old bones along by the side of Falstaff's heaving mountain of flesh, and hears his " We have heard the chimes at midnight, Master Shallow," he warms into reminiscence, and spectral wine and women and cudgel-play and all the wild nights of youth come to life. And Master Silence, for the thousandth time, hears the tale again (he knows it well—" That's fifty-five years ago," he prompts), and fixes his bucolic gaze, in which awe, envy, fear, and admiration are mingled, upon this rollicking head of the family. Even that unknown idol, goodman Puff of Barson, probably could not show such a past.

Silence is one of those characters (Slender and Sir Andrew Aguecheek are two others) that only Shakespeare could bring on the stage and leave us convinced of their reality. As Hazlitt has remarked : " In point of understanding and attainments, Shallow sinks low enough ; and yet his cousin Silence is a foil to him ; he is the shadow of a shade, glimmers on the very edge of downright imbecility, and totters on the brink of nothing." Revolving round the great roaring sun of Falstaff, we discover, in the far outer spaces, this dim fantastic planet of a Shallow, and yet this poor cinder in the darkness has its satellite, Silence, its faint little moon. So slight is Silence's demand upon life that he can bask even in the meagre bleak sunshine of his cousin, the Justice, and hear things even in this orchard that add colour to his dreams. Nay, when there has been an unusually liberal allowance of sack at supper, in honour of the great Sir John's presence, he can not only sit in the garden with the rest but can break into song without encouragement, lifting his faint voice like some roistering sparrow, some care-free sprawling field-mouse. Should

Falstaff, with ironic appraisement, declare that he had not thought Master Silence had been a man of such mettle, he can reply " Who, I ? I have been merry twice and once ere now," and thus flash a light upon his Sahara of an existence through which has trickled a tiny wasted brook of sack and song. Poor Silence ! —we leave him, drowned by the last bumper, stunned by the fiery rhetoric of Pistol, asleep under the apple trees. He is not carried to the triumph in London, and so, at least, is saved a night in the Fleet. Shallow kept that adventure to himself, and perhaps it was worth all the thousand pounds he lost to Sir John when he returned to amaze Cousin Silence again over the pippins and caraways in Glostershire.

Into these grotesques, these dim rural shades, Shakespeare has breathed the life that he could spare for all his creatures. No one but him could have written that dialogue between Shallow and Silence when we first meet them, that dialogue which Hazlitt and others have so rightly singled out for praise, a passage of talk so ludicrous and yet so commonplace, so characteristic of the speakers and yet so touched with universality. The fussy, vain, trivial, prattling Justice, determined to talk and yet not able to keep to one point for two sentences together, never forgetting, whatever he is saying, his own importance, the figure he cuts in the eyes of his companion ;

and Silence, so proud of being where he is and of talking so familiarly to his great relative, so foolish and simple ; and both of them, in their vanity and simplicity, so very human that their silly talk lights up, for a moment, the whole strange business of this life :

SHALLOW. Certain, 'tis certain ; very sure, very sure : death, as the Psalmist saith, is certain to all ; all shall die. How a good yoke of bullocks at Stamford fair ?

SILENCE. Truly, cousin, I was not there.

SHALLOW. Death is certain. Is old Double of your town living yet ?

SILENCE. Dead, sir.

SHALLOW. Jesu, Jesu, dead !—'a drew a good bow ; and dead !—'a shot a fine shoot : John o' Gaunt loved him well, and betted much money on his head. Dead! —'a would have clapped i' the clout at twelve score ; and carried you a forehand shaft a fourteen and fourteen and a half, that it would have done a man's heart good to see. How a score of ewes now ?

SILENCE. Thereafter as they be : a score of good ewes may be worth ten pounds.

SHALLOW. And is old Double dead ?

Let us leave the two old men, nodding and talking, creasing their wintry faces in the sunshine. They have said everything, foolish as they are. Even old Double, who shot a fine shoot and was loved by John o' Gaunt, is dead, and a score of good ewes may be worth ten pounds, and death is certain. This is the world's news, and this

D

is the world's history, and all the philosophers have told us little more.

2

As a purely literary figure that has seized hold upon men's imagination, aroused their curiosity and won their affection, Falstaff has only two rivals or superiors, namely, Hamlet, the great figure of tragedy, and Don Quixote, the great figure of ironic tragi-comedy or romance ; and in his own sphere of the comic, he has no rival.   So much has been written about him that any new study cannot be simply an essay in interpretation, a lightning sketch portrait, as the other chapters of this volume are, but must inevitably be a criticism of previous interpretations. The best of these are Maurice Morgann's *Essay on the Dramatic Character of Sir John Falstaff* and *The Rejection of Falstaff* in Mr. A. C. Bradley's Oxford Lectures on Poetry.   The worst are everywhere.   Among commentators of any importance, the account of Falstaff by Gervinus, who does not appear to have had a glimmer of humour and should have kept out of the fat knight's company, must take one of the highest places as a monument of obtuseness and critical density.   It is Gervinus who tells us, while shaking his head over Falstaff's incorrigible coarseness and lewdness, that the little page was given to him in order that the tenderly nurtured

lad might have a refining influence, instead of which
—alas !—he is himself corrupted.   Gervinus, too, is
one of those simple souls who imagine that Falstaff's
moments of " sighing and grief " are moments of real
repentance, that the knight would be good if he could
but is somewhat weak-willed and easily led astray.   Why
persons who are willing to admit that Falstaff is a great
humorist should insist upon taking every remark he makes
as a serious literal statement is a mystery.   But equally
strange is the fact that the persons who are always pro-
claiming Shakespeare's genius as a dramatic artist are
more often than not the very persons who are always
discovering his personal opinions in the mouths of his
characters.   If we read through the various interpretations and appreciations we shall find there are at least
half-a-dozen different Falstaffs, ranging from the bloated
buffoon to a kind of comic philosopher who, as it were,
evolves his sack and sugar from his inner consciousness.
But these are not, of course, creatures of any substance
but only shadows thrown on the minds of different
critics by the single figure of the play, who exists
for us only in so many pages of dialogue and a few,
probably traditional, stage directions.   And we can
probably clear away a good many common misconcep-
tions if we begin by seeing Falstaff against the background of the play, as one out of many characters who

has, whether he likes it or not, to play his part in the action.

Shakespeare had the broad lines of the two parts of *Henry IV.* laid down for him by history, supported by tradition. Prince Hal had to have bad companions. Such companions had to be amusing in order that the scenes in which they figured should be welcome as comic relief to the severely historical world of court and camp, statecraft and strategy, in which the main action should go forward. If they should have a leader who would prove himself to be a comic figure of the first order, so much the better for the play. So Falstaff comes into being. But Shakespeare, most modern critics argue, having once conceived the knight, worked only too well, with the result that this comic character is, as it were, too big to be squeezed back again into the plot. He has to be cast off with the rest of the bad companions, once Henry is king, so that at the end of the play, when we see him and his followers hurried off to the Fleet at Henry's express command, we are left in doubt and dismay, our sympathies go out not to the newly crowned " hero " but to the old rascal, so ruthlessly toppled out of his dreams, whom one critic at least, Hazlitt, has frankly called " the better man." All this is so familiar that there is no need to dwell upon it. If Shakespeare put forward Prince Hal as a conventional " hero," whose

every action we are intended to applaud, he appears to
have muddled his work. Either Falstaff should have
been less fascinating or Henry should have acted differently. But all this is assuming what we have no right
to assume, namely, that Shakespeare expected us to " take
sides " and that the play ended in one of those reconcilia-
tions that suddenly transform this world into a paradise
of poetic justice. Actually what Shakespeare did do
was to show us what happened, a very different thing.
And what happened is exactly what does happen in this
world, a planet in which Shakespeare was interested to
the exclusion of any interest in more distant and nebulous
realms. It is on record that a young man led a wild
life and then suddenly found himself called upon to hold
an extremely responsible position, which he proceeded
to do with all the ruthless fervour of the converted.
You cannot be King of England and also second-in-
command of the Boar's Head Tavern, Eastcheap. If
you are to be King, to shoulder enormous responsibilities,
to talk weightily of honour on all public occasions, then
Falstaff, delightful Falstaff, who happens to be the avowed
enemy of all responsibilities, to whom honour is but one
of many targets, must go. When we see him in the
new and searching light of such responsibilities, of such
notions as honour, he will appear so monstrous that not
only shall we be not reluctant to let him go, driving him

away freely, we may be suddenly resentful, apparently angry at his presumption but really angry at the thought of what appears to us our former weakness, and so not only do we tell him to remove himself from our presence, but in a later flash of resentment we order him to the Fleet.

It has been said, more than once, that Shakespeare, realising that his Falstaff of the First Part is too engaging and that we must be ready to approve his final rejection, deliberately blackens him in the Second Part. This is a mistake. Absurd as it is to act the magistrate with this great comic figure, drawing up a list of his misdemeanours in the order of their importance, we have only to think of the action of the two parts to realise that there is nothing in the theory. Falstaff's gravest offence is probably the one which first shows him in action, the highway robbery. What Shakespeare did do, towards the end of the Second Part, was to emphasise the fact that Falstaff as a companion and confidant of a serious ruler was impossible, a fact that was obvious throughout but perhaps needed to be emphasised in order that the issue should be clear. When Pistol rushes in with the great news and Falstaff talks as if the realm were already in his pocket, it is plain that disaster is imminent. Henry has to choose between kingship and Falstaff, and being, at heart, a very ambitious young man, he naturally chooses the former. It is inevitable, and, as we know, something like it actually happened. His conduct at the conclusion of the play is perfectly natural. Being a converted rake, very conscious of his improvement, it is natural that he should talk like a prig. He never was at any time a gentleman. His terms too, to Falstaff, are not too severe : Falstaff is banished from his presence, on a pension, until he has reformed, when he may expect advancement. The last painful stroke, coming suddenly out of the blue, the order to imprison Falstaff and his company in the Fleet, is probably partly the expression of a sudden resentment and partly the result of a desire to add force to his speech to the bewildered knight. Shakespeare—it cannot be repeated too often—shows us what happened, what was inevitable under such circumstances and with such characters, and leaves the situation to make its own impression. And our attitude towards it is determined by our cast of mind. This is why the critics have differed so widely. If we are romantic Hotspurs or solemn Lancasters, we shall rejoice that the air is now cleared of its Falstaffian malodours, that honour and responsibility and the like have now the stage to themselves. Behind the bent, receding back of Sir John, we shall read a little moral lesson, as Gervinus does. If, on the other hand, we delight in sack and sugar, mirth and ease, and revel in the unfamiliar sense of freedom that is the very atmosphere of Falstaff, compared with which the world into which Henry enters, the world of statecraft and battle, is something forbiddingly angular and hard, then the end of the play will leave us resentful or depressed, as if we had been present at a piece of rank injustice.   And if we can enter, with sympathy, into both worlds, but find ourselves torn between them, knowing that they are incompatible, that we cannot have our cake and eat it, then we shall be neither complacent nor resentful but will find ourselves at once quickened, by our dramatic sympathy, and yet thoughtful, dubious, touched by the old irony of things.

Like most really great figures and great works of art, Falstaff has an equally successful appeal on many different levels.   That is why there are so many Falstaffs, all heartily praised as great comic characters.   As our sense of humour and character mellows and grows more subtle, so too the Falstaff to whom we inevitably return changes with us ;   we begin with a bloated old buffoon, whose gluttony, cowardice, lying are on such a colossal scale that we cannot help being amused by them ;   we end with the comic genius, busy dramatising himself, as it were, that may be discovered in the pages of Morgann and Mr. A. C. Bradley.   Don Quixote has had a similar history, for he too can be enjoyed at all levels and changes with the reader.   That is why discussions of such things as Falstaff's apparent cowardice and love of boasting, though both interesting and amusing, are not really important. If we think that real cowardice and boasting are much funnier than pretended cowardice and boasting, if, in short, we prefer a real butt to an apparent one, then we shall continue to say that Falstaff is simply a coward and a boaster. His character is, as it were, a test of our sense of humour. Actually if he had been nothing more than what is discovered in him by somewhat naïve critics, most of us would have tired of him long ago : a fatter Parolles, a Bobadil with wit, could never have exercised such dominion over us. Thus the Falstaff of the stage is only the creature of the first level, and this is why he has ceased to interest many persons who find him enchanting in the library. Mr. A. B. Walkley, for example, discussing bores on the stage, has not hesitated to include Falstaff amongst them. He is one of our greatest English masterpieces of wit and humour and human character, Mr. Walkley remarks, but only " to read, to imagine in one's mind's eye, to turn over on one's tongue ; but on the stage his eternal paunch gets in the way. His wheezings and puffings, his gurgling potations, and all the ' business ' that actors think indispensable to a grossly fat man are to me mere ugliness and the occasion of *ennui*." This confession by a dramatic critic, who is not grinding the axe of any particular theory of character but is merely examining his reactions in the theatre, is valuable because it proves that once we have passed the stage at which Falstaff is a mere butt and have recognised that he is a great humorist, then a naïve presentation of the character, designed to appeal to those who see nothing but the fat buffoon in him, is not only not acceptable but definitely irritating or fatiguing, a dull travesty of a remarkable personage, as if—let us say—Dr. Johnson should be played by a circus clown. Nevertheless Falstaff owes his predominant position among comic figures to the fact that in him there meet the clown that delights the crowd, who love a person to laugh at ; and the subtle character that engages the philosopher, who loves a person to laugh with. The first is a tribute to Shakespeare as a writer for his own theatre, the second is a tribute to his power of subtle characterisation, and the whole figure, displaying so many facets as the lights of different intelligences flash upon him and never failing to win your laughter and applause whatever your idea of the comic may be, is an example of his creator's amazing dramatic genius. He sets Falstaff walking and talking down the centuries, and though they may be ages of reason or ages of romance, they call for the biggest armchair, place him in their midst, and will not let him go.

We have said that the two most important interpretations of Falstaff's character are those by Maurice Morgann and Mr. A. C. Bradley, and from each of these critics we can take a key that will unlock one part of the secret Morgann, who throughout concentrates upon the incongruities to be found in Falstaff's character, tells us what Falstaff is, and, in part, why we find him so fascinating : " He is a man at once young and old, enterprising and fat, a dupe and a wit, harmless and wicked, weak in principle and resolute by constitution, cowardly in appearance and brave in reality, a knave without malice, a liar without deceit, and a knight, a gentleman, and a soldier, without either dignity, decency, or honour." Mr. Bradley tells us what Falstaff does : " The bliss of freedom gained in humour is the essence of Falstaff. His humour is not directed only or chiefly against obvious absurdities ; he is the enemy of everything that would interfere with his ease, and therefore of anything serious, and especially of everything respectable and moral. For these things impose limits and obligations, and make us the subjects of old father antic the law, and the categorical imperative, and our station and its duties, and conscience, and reputation, and other people's opinions, and all sorts of nuisances. I say he is therefore their enemy ; but I do him wrong ; to say that he is their enemy implies that he regards them as serious and recognises their power, when in truth he refuses to recognise them at all. They are to him absurd ; and to reduce a thing *ad absurdum* is to reduce it to nothing and to walk about free and rejoicing." The two together, incongruity and freedom, give us the secret of Falstaff, and indeed of the comic world in which he is the largest and most notable figure. If we want any further explanation of his power of delighting, with a few exceptions, all those with whom he comes into contact, we may find it in his own words : " Men of all sorts take a pride to gird at me : the brain of this foolish-compounded clay, man, is not able to invent any thing that tends to laughter, more than I invent or is invented on me : I am not only witty in myself, but the cause that wit is in other men." And these words of his are still sounding in our ears when he furnishes us with an example of his power, for in the conversation that follows with the Chief Justice, the very embodiment of all the things that Falstaff will not recognise, we can watch the severity of that official gradually thaw, in spite of the impudence of Falstaff's humour, and can hear his speeches catching something of the tone of Falstaff's until he quits the stage in high good humour with himself as a wit, a weakness of judges from that day to this. The only persons that Falstaff cannot conquer are those who are cold, severe, and obtuse, liking wit not at all, not even in themselves, such as the young Prince John of Lancaster, one of Falstaff's most notable failures—" Good faith, this same young sober-blooded boy doth not love me ; nor a man cannot make him laugh." Falstaff himself has no illusions about his power

There is no mystery, as some critics would have us suppose, about the appeal of such comic characters as Falstaff. Their crimes and vices, such as they are (and they are never very grave), have little or no effect upon us ; they are so distant from us that we can regard them without moral indignation ; it is not *our* sack they drink nor *our* money they borrow or steal or " convey " ; it is no more possible to work ourselves up into a state of moral indignation over them than it is for us to grow angry at the thought of all the bandits existing in the remoter provinces of China, or tearful over the sexual laxity of the aborigines. On the other hand, though such fellows do not borrow *our* money and get drunk in *our* houses, so that their little weaknesses do not trouble us, it is for us, in the last resort, that these amusing rascals go through their various antics ; their depredations are distant in time and space, but their jokes are here and now. Thus we can afford to be indulgent and to encourage them. It is often forgotten that Falstaff, after all, stands for something that is good in itself. He is the embodiment of masculine comradeship, ease, and merriment. He turns the whole world into the smoking-room of a club. He is the supreme example of the clubbable man. That word brings Dr. Johnson to our minds, and Dr Johnson was a moralist by nature, and a somewhat severe moralist, but he loved company and ease and mirth, loved them all the more because there was in him a decided streak of melancholy and despondency. He does not understand Falstaff, but how he enjoys him, in spite of himself—" But *Falstaff* unimitated, unimitable *Falstaff*, how shall I describe thee ? " he begins, throwing his judicial manner, the wig and robes of his office as a critic, to the winds. It is the clubbable man in him that is responding to the immortal master of the revels, the patron saint of all who love to assemble a few choice spirits, golden lads, shut the doors upon gravity and decorum, duty, and responsibility, and fleet the time in unbuttoned ease. All this is very masculine, and we have no reason to be surprised that women do not take kindly to Falstaff, however lively their sense of humour, for it is not only that he seems to them a gross old man, but that they suspect in him, and suspect rightly, their arch-enemy who would, if he had his way, undermine all their good work. What is he but that old rascal whose conversation, which John, in his tiresome way, finds so fascinating, keeps a husband from his hearth and bed, night after night at the club ? He is the wild-bird crying outside the domestic cage, the siren-song from the convivial circle, the tavern and the club. And just as women, however he may stir their laughter, cannot help disliking him, so men, unless they are completely ossified by rules and regulations, cannot help liking him, personifying as he does the supreme satisfaction of an impulse that cannot be denied without pain and loss.

We see the scenes that Falstaff dominates and makes his own against an ideal background for them, a world of statecraft and war, policy and cabals, of men whose armour seems to have grown upon them like a skin, so angular and stiff, so lacking in spontaneity are most of these barons.   After spending some time in the company of these personages, we return to Falstaff with a glorious sense of freedom and spontaneity ; the natural man is loose again ; it is as if we ourselves had suddenly doffed our armour.   And that indeed is what we have done, for we have doffed the armour of duties and obligations and rights and responsibilities.   All the secret fears, the reservations, the conflicts are suddenly dropped from our minds and we can step out as free as the wind.   We can loll unbuttoned, with the world no longer pressing down our Atlas shoulders, but now our footstool or, if necessary, our football.   This is the influence of Falstaff who has conjured all existence into matter for a jest. All the common standards disappear at one wave of his hand ; no chain can be forged for him ; not even the bonds of the flesh can confine him because with him they are not bonds but either something to be enjoyed, with

such enormous gusto that cups of sack and capons seem
alone worth living for, or something that is easily transformed, by an amazingly adroit wit, into yet another
joke.   Thus, to take a simple example, Falstaff's enormous girth troubles him not at all ; it becomes his ally ;
he uses it to gain a humorous superiority over smaller
persons, such as Prince Hal and Poins and Justice Shallow,
who are tailor's-yards, bow-cases, men made out of a
cheese-paring ; and he also uses it as fresh matter on
which to exercise his humorous fancy, so that when he
is with the tiny page he can say " I do here walk before
thee like a sow that hath overwhelm'd all her litter but
one."   But so confident is he in his unmatched powers
that not only can he turn every occasion into a jest, but
he can and does deliberately complicate matters, contrive
that things shall be almost as bad as they can for him,
knowing that he can escape in triumph, dissolving everything into laughter.   Compared with him, we are all
slaves.   Out of his incongruous self and the incongruity
that he is quick to perceive everywhere, he has contrived
to build up a kingdom of his own, a Cloud-Cuckoodom,
that exists in its own right and has its own consistency.
There, all the restraints of this life are only so many
little playthings ; old father antic the law is our butt ;
we have no secrets and can never be disillusioned ; we
are the triumphant supper-party behind the scenes of

life ; the curse of Adam has been blown away.   Throned
in this kingdom, Falstaff is seemingly invulnerable ;
what would be weaknesses to other men become sources
of strength to him ; every predicament, every crisis, is
but the beginning of a fresh triumph ; every arrow shot
from the bow of circumstance he catches in his hand and
suddenly twists into some ludicrous shape, only to waken
more laughter ; he has frankly entertained the animal
in himself, banishing the solemn dreams of our species
in order to do so, and now, behold, the animal is no
longer there—for he is throned like a god, enjoying a
freedom, a dominion over the sad necessities, compared
with which our common existence is a term in the galleys
What does it matter that he is old and fat and ever thirsty
and reduced to begging from old women, that his name
is tarnished and his reputation an evil odour among the
godly ?   He has escaped from the machinery of our moral
and social order, does not obey or even recognise its
rules, but has long since passed into his own kingdom,
there attended by a host of fiery, nimble, and delectable
shapes, born of fancy and sack.   All our criticism passes
him by.   And so inward and searching is his humour,
his mind so free from all common subterfuges and disguises, that however we may point to his devotion to
sack, his great belly, his ancient lechery, his gross, palpable,
open lies, we cannot laugh *at* him because he has every-

where forestalled us, pointed the way, and laughed first
himself, so that willy-nilly we are compelled to laugh
with him and thus enter his own kingdom.   He seems
to have accepted all the facts, he has not buried away a
single impulse, and would appear to have achieved what
all men wish to achieve, a synthesis, and so become master
of life.   Small wonder that he seems invulnerable.

So far we have only considered the two parts of
Henry IV., but there is another play to be considered,
Henry V.   And it is what we hear of Falstaff in *Henry V.*,
when we learn that he is nearing his end mainly because
" the King hath run bad humours on the knight " and
" his heart is fracted and corroborate," it is this and not
the end of *Henry IV.* that largely determines our attitude
of sympathy towards Falstaff and resentment against
Henry.   And this tells us why Falstaff was not invulnerable, why his kingdom suddenly wasted away like some
cloud-city in the sunset.   The usual explanation is that
Falstaff, as Dowden puts it, " endeavours to corruscate
away the realities of life," but that hard fact was too much
for him in the end.   Now this is true in essence, but it
is a thought too sweeping and is liable to give a wrong
impression.   If Falstaff answered in every single particular to the description we have already given of him,
if he were exactly what he imagined himself to be, no
such disaster could have taken place.   What is the worst

he has to face ? Prince Hal, who has been one of his companions for some years, though obviously for only a comparatively short period of Falstaff's life, is now king, but, instead of loading his old friend with honours and allowing him to do what he pleases, he banishes him on a small allowance and tells him to reform himself. The imprisonment in the Fleet is obviously only temporary. It is all very disappointing, but, after all, it is only one joke in a series of such things that we have agreed to call life ; Falstaff has weathered and contrived to enjoy worse storms than this ; if the King has turned virtuous, so much the worse for him ; there are other good fellows in the world, and there are still cups of sack and capons. In short, Falstaff has lost a boon-companion and, with him, a number of expectations that he has humour enough not to worry about, and he has gained an allowance. He enjoyed life when the prince was still in the nursery and can enjoy it again now that he is in the council-chamber. Why, then, this utter collapse ? Why has the apparently invulnerable system of our comic philo-sopher crumbled to dust at the touch of this single stroke of ill fortune ? The answer, of course, is to be found in Pistol's remark that " his heart is fracted and corro-borate." Falstaff has been doing something he has had no right to do, something for which his humour has failed to provide, he has long been feeling a very genuine affection for Henry. He loves the man. And now he is utterly repudiated, spoken to with cold contempt, and though he could have laughed away his ruined hopes, the thousand pounds he owes to Shallow, and the rest, this he cannot laugh away and all is in the dust. Life has only laughed once at Master Falstaff, without his bidding, but it has laughed last, and now his mouth is choked with ashes. Just as there fell upon Siegfried, bathing in the dragon's blood, a single leaf that left him vulnerable, so too there fell upon Falstaff this love of his for the prince, and through that vulnerable mark the arrow shot home that sent him shaking to his bed, to fumble with the sheets, babble of green fields, and make an end of it all. That Falstaff's kingdom, in which he walked free as air, was an illusion cannot be denied ; the cold daylight had to stream some time through those rich painted tapestries of his mind, but it would have been well if the first rent could have been made by some other hand and not by that of the one man he really loved. But so it was, and so, of course, it was bound to be ; no other hand could have scattered his kingdom ; this comic hero, like so many heroes of epic and tragedy, was betrayed by his heart, the last incongruous and ironic stroke in his life and the only one that mastered him. Henry went forward to Agincourt and became a popular hero, a figure for patriots in a noisy mood. Falstaff, who had the larger heart and the better mind, went forward into immortality and has since gained undreamed-of honours, presiding in spirit wherever there have been boon companions, ease and laughter. He was rejected once, but he has never been rejected again. Whenever the choice spirits of this world have put the day's work out of their minds and have seated themselves at the table of goodfellowship and humour, there has been an honoured place at the board for Sir John Falstaff, in whose gigantic shadow we can laugh at this life and laugh at ourselves, and so, divinely careless, sit like gods for an hour.

PARSON ADAMS

THE real hero of Fielding's *Joseph Andrews* is Mr. Abraham Adams. Everybody knows how this story was begun as a burlesque of Richardson's *Pamela*, Joseph being the brother of Pamela and footman to Lady Booby, who pursues him in much the same way that her nephew, Mr. B., pursues Pamela ; and how the burlesque was dropped, though not entirely, after the first few chapters. Joseph begins by being a stick with which Fielding could beat Richardson, and even when the parody comes to an end and the real story begins, Joseph, though nominally the hero, still remains a stick. It is his friend, mentor, and companion of his travels, Parson Adams, who occupies the middle of the stage. His entrance upon the scene, with some assistance from Mrs. Slipslop and a few minor personages, sets the tale in motion. He is at once a notable comic character and a heroic figure, and he differs from most other comic characters of his stature in being not fundamentally absurd but only absurd in certain situations. He is not a conscious humorist, and, indeed, has practically no sense of humour; with a sense of humour he would be less innocent, more suspicious of his fellow-creatures, and would contrive to keep out of the hundred-and-one scrapes into which he falls so easily. He appears at first to be one of those comic figures who are mere butts, targets for the jests of their authors. We see him land into misadventure after misadventure; never was there a more undignified priest; he wanders from inn to inn without the means to pay his bills; he is beaten and cudgelled, swindled and mocked, through chapter after chapter; he is drenched with pigs' blood and other unsavoury liquids, trampled in the mire of a pigsty, brought to bed (innocently, we must confess) with Mrs. Slipslop: there is no end to the indignities he is made to suffer. Yet he is no mere butt. Though we see how his innocence brings about one ludicrous mishap after another, we not only like him more and more, we also respect him more and more. Even during a first reading of the story, he soon towers above all the other characters and lays a successful claim to the greater part of our attention; and once we know the book, we await his appearance with impatience. He is of the comic-heroic brood of Don Quixote, whose innocent eyes and much-belaboured carcases seem to us, after a time, a mute but terrible comment upon a world that took them so lightly. It is easy to conceive such figures, but it is difficult to give them life, to make them real and personal ; and it is not the least of Fielding's triumphs that Parson Adams, as Mr. Saintsbury once remarked, " is a good deal more real than half the parsons who preached last Sunday, and a good deal more personal."

Few humorous characters have been so heartily praised as Parson Adams ; critic after critic has added to the chorus of praise, and his various oddities, his absent-mindedness and innocent vanity, have been noted in a score of famous volumes. When Fielding formally introduces Mr. Abraham Adams to us at the beginning of *Joseph Andrews*, we are told that he was an excellent scholar, master of several ancient and modern tongues, that " he had applied many years to the most severe study, and had treasured up a fund of learning rarely to be met with in a university " ; and further, that he was "a man of good sense, good parts, and good nature ; but was at the same time as entirely ignorant of the ways of the world as an infant just entered into it could possibly be." He was generous, friendly, and brave, to an excess, and very simple, absent-minded, and unsuspecting. Further, he lived in a remote country curacy, with a wife and six children, on " a handsome income of twenty-three pounds a-year." Here, it seems, is a figure very familiar in comic literature, that of the absent-minded scholar, the innocent pedant, who formed a stock subject for jokes in Ancient Greece and is still to be found, putting his umbrella to bed and then standing in the hall himself, in the comic papers. But Fielding takes this stock figure, breathes life into it, sets it in motion, and gives it an individuality. He sends him wandering down that old road which is the very backbone of great comic literature, that road which has seen so many glorious innocents and their happy folly, and brings him into adventure after adventure. With a bagful of sermons and nine shillings and threepence-halfpenny in his pocket, Adams arrives, it will be remembered, at the inn where Joseph Andrews, who has been robbed and wounded, is lying in bed. The good man is on his way to London to publish three volumes of his sermons, out of which he hopes, in his innocence, to make a considerable sum of money. After paying for Joseph as well as himself, he finds he has very little money left and determines to borrow three guineas from the landlord—" on ample security." The latter is agreeable and only wishes to see the security :

Upon which Adams, pointing to his saddle-bag, told him, with a face and voice full of solemnity, " that there were in that bag no less than nine volumes of manuscript sermons, as well worth a hundred pounds as a shilling was worth twelve-pence, and that he would deposit one of the volumes in his hands by way of pledge ; not doubting but that he would have the honesty to return it on his repayment of the money ; for otherwise he must be a very great loser, seeing that every volume would at least bring him ten pounds, as he had been informed by a neighbouring clergyman in the country ; for," said he, " as to my own part, having never yet dealt in printing, I do not pretend to ascertain the exact value of such things."

The landlord, however, finds the sermons no better security than Master Dombledom found Bardolph, and so he refuses the loan.   After this disappointment, poor Adams has a further one, for he is given to understand by Parson Barnabas and his friend, the bookseller, that sermons, unless of heterodox tendency, are a drug on the market.   This expert opinion, however, does not entirely destroy his faith, and he is only prevented from setting out for London by the unwelcome discovery, made by Joseph, that the nine volumes of sermons have been left behind at home, Mrs. Adams having packed shirts and other useful articles in their stead.   There is nothing for it but to return home with Joseph, having one horse and one shilling between them.   After some further adventures, at the very next inn at which he and Joseph, who have now joined Mrs. Slipslop's party, put up, the impulsive Adams, having struck the surly inn-keeper, who will not allow his wife to attend to Joseph's bad leg, begins that free fight in which a pan full of hogs' blood plays such a prominent part.   A little later, after a great struggle, he rescues Fanny from the hands of a ravisher, and then both of them, having been discovered by a gang of villagers, are hauled before the justice, only to be released after a most amusing examination. Early the next morning, while sitting before the fire in a tavern, they hear the voice of Joseph, whom Adams contrived to lose before he met with Fanny, singing a song, and this is the great moment when Fanny faints and Adams, in his agitation, hurls his beloved Aeschylus into the fire. Penniless and with the lovely Fanny a temptation to every lustful fox-hunting lord of the manor they are likely to encounter, Adams and his two young friends set out for home, only to fall into mishap after mishap, and have adventures too numerous and complicated to be chronicled in this place.

Some characters are best discussed and others are best shown in action, and Adams being one of the latter it is more profitable to show him in relation to his experiences than merely to talk about him. His adventures, though for the most part ludicrous, are of various kinds. Some, the most superficial, come very near to the rough-and-tumble affairs, the horse-play and practical jokes, in which Smollett delighted and in which Fielding only took moderate pleasure. Even the lightest have some relation to character. Quite early in the narrative, for example, there is an account of how Adams, walking by himself in the dark, wades through a pond because he has failed to look over a hedge and notice that there is a footpath that would have taken him round ; and how that, even then, when he is wet through, he sits down on a stile to read his Aeschylus and never notices, until a passer-by, replying to his question, points it out to him, that there is an inn a few yards away.   There is, of course, nothing very subtle about this, which shows us the absent-minded scholar of comic tradition.   On the same level, though rather more diverting, is that episode towards the end of the book, that chapter of accidents at night which is one of the stock pieces of comic business in *picaresque* literature.   Adams, Joseph, and Fanny are staying at Lady Booby's, and another guest, one Beau Didapper, who has conceived a passion for Fanny, resolves to visit her bedroom in the dead of night.   Unfortunately, it is Mrs. Slipslop and not Fanny that he visits.   Adams, hearing the noise and suspecting a rape, rushes in, and in the darkness imagines Slipslop to be the man and the little Beau to be the woman.   The latter escapes and Adams grapples with Slipslop, only to be discovered, in a very compromising situation, by the whole household. Explanations follow, and the good parson marches off to his bedroom, but instead of turning to the right he turns to the left, unknowingly enters Fanny's bedroom and actually gets into the same bed without disturbing her (she is thoroughly exhausted by her adventures of the previous night), and without discovering the mistake himself. There he is found early next morning by Joseph, whose faith in the good man is put to a very severe test. Such chapters of accidents are very familiar to students of the *picaresque*, and all that need be said of this one is that there is some slight relation to character in it (for Adams' first action is the result of his impulsive gallantry and his second the result of his absent-mindedness), but that it is not enough to make the episode anything more than a piece of comic business of a very familiar type. Smollett could bustle through such rough-and-tumble business just as well, if not better (for he enjoyed it more) ; but when we come to some of the other incidents in which Adams figures we leave Smollett far behind ; we come, indeed, to the great Fielding.

In his Preface to *Joseph Andrews* (a little essay that is full of meat) Fielding gives us his view of the ridiculous and also mentions the character of Adams, but unfortunately he does not bring the two together. We are told that the only source of the true ridiculous is affectation, and that affectation proceeds from one of two causes, vanity or hypocrisy. We are also told, at the end of the Preface, that Adams is " the most glaring " character in the book, one not to be found " in any book now extant," " a character of perfect simplicity," whose "goodness of heart will recommend him to the good-natured"; and so forth.   There is nothing here about affectation, that only source of the true ridiculous, nothing here about vanity and hypocrisy; and yet Adams is clearly the chief comic figure in the book.   The fact is, of course, that Adams, in Fielding's view, stands outside the true ridiculous, which is something nearer to satire or burlesque than it is to our later view of humour. Adams is a comic-heroic figure; he is not only extremely lovable, but also, in the last resort, he commands our respect.   The moralities in the book, you may say, are in his keeping, and despite his eccentricities they could not be in better hands.   When Lady Booby, who is nearly all-powerful in her own village, tells him that he must not publish the banns between Joseph and Fanny, he defies her; and afterwards becomes even more heroic by giving the same answer to his wife.   When the hunting squire persuades him to accept hospitality and then encourages the rest of the company to play tricks on the poor bedraggled parson, Adams, after submitting for a time with great good humour, stands up and rebukes the company manfully.   The speech is entirely in character and has one or two passages that are half-comical, half-pathetic, as, for example, when Adams exclaims :

". . . My appearance might very well persuade you that your invitation was an act of charity, though in

reality we were very well provided ; yes, sir, if we had
had an hundred miles to travel, we had sufficient to bear
our expenses in a noble manner." (At which words he
produced the half-guinea which was found in the basket.)
" I do not show you this out of ostentation of riches, but
to convince you I speak truth."

There is all the speaker's innocence in that " ostentation
of riches." But the whole speech, which is far too long
to be quoted here, is a fine, sturdy rebuke, and not all the
reek and muck of horse-ponds and pigsties, the sight of
torn cassocks and dirty night-caps, can take away the
essential dignity and manliness of him that made it. He
is the Church Militant.

But this is not the reason why we like him so well ;
nor was it Fielding's reason. Fielding, as Raleigh once
pointed out, is, like most men of his time, a moralist,
you might call him a romantic moralist, for he makes it
his business to stress the fact that there is nothing so good
in the world as a good will ; "goodness of heart," to
use his own phrase, is opposed to the formal compliance
with a moral code. " Against the pedantry of the formal
moralist," Raleigh remarked, " Fielding delights to hurl
his satire. He can clear away in a moment all the
'splendid rubbish' that covers up a character, and expose
its inherent rottenness or meanness. He never tires of
showing how a base-minded man may cover himself

with formal righteousness, and how a scapegrace may be good at heart." Over and above his obvious qualities as a story-teller, it is this ever-present contrast between native impulse towards good and mere conformity to the prevailing code, along with his profound knowledge of human nature, his delight in the pursuit of vanity and in the little ironies of life, that gives Fielding's work that massiveness and intellectual strength which is more obvious on the third or fourth time of reading than it is on the first. And it might be added that just because he is a part of this massive intellectual structure, Adams is a great character, but not, strictly speaking, a great *comic* character ; for the greatest comic characters are engendered during a moral holiday, they soar above such matters as vanity and affectation and the complication of motives, and Fielding never took a moral holiday and had too much solid prose in his composition ever to rise into the realm of pure fantasy and absurdity. He took care, of course, to dower Adams with that " goodness of heart " in full measure, and having done this, he did not scruple to laugh at *his* little vanities and affectations. Adams himself is a moralist whose heart often says one thing while his code says another, but unlike most of Fielding's personages, while his code is sound, his heart is even sounder, so that any difference between the two only makes plain some weakness or other in the ethics that Adams preaches so energetically at various moments in the narrative. His little vanities, inevitable in so warm-hearted a man as this, are so innocent that, led by Fielding, we laugh at them only as we might laugh at the antics of a child, and we love him no less, perhaps even more, on their account ; yet beneath our author's ironic presentment of such things there is to be discovered a certain note of warning that might be interpreted in some such words as these : Here, in this creature, as innocent as a child, pure in heart and flawless in his motives, there is still the weakness of our erring humanity ; elaborate self-deception and vanity ; and as for you, now priding yourself on your superior sagacity, examine your heart to discover whether there is that in you which will reduce your affectation and restless vanity to nothing but food for easy, kindly laughter ; and if not. . . . And the author's irony plays about this grotesque but lovable figure, so untiring in its charity, like harmless summer lightning, illuminating but not striking it, secure as it is in the sanctuary of the good will.

With this figure in our memory, we may turn back to the narrative, examine this episode or that, and discover how admirably Fielding has done his work. How excellent are some of the single remarks, such things as this :

Darkness had now overspread the hemisphere, when Fanny whispered Joseph that she begged to rest herself a little ; for that she was so tired she could walk no farther. Joseph immediately prevailed with Parson Adams, who was as brisk as a bee, to stop. He had no sooner seated himself than he lamented the loss of his dear Aeschylus ; but was a little comforted when reminded that, if he had it in his possession, he could not see to read.

Who could forget, having once read, that description of Adams at Wilson's house, when the latter relates his mournful history, and particularly enlarges on the subject of vanity—" that worst of passions " ? —

My second remark was (Wilson is speaking), that vanity is the worst of passions, and more apt to contaminate the mind than any other : for as selfishness is much more general than we please to allow it, so it is natural to hate and envy those who stand between us and the good we desire.   Now, in lust and ambition, these are few ; and even in avarice we find many who are no obstacles to our pursuits ; but the vain man seeks pre-eminence ; and everything which is excellent or praiseworthy in another renders him the mark of his antipathy.—Adams now began to fumble in his pockets, and soon cried out, " O la ! I have it not about me."—Upon this the gentleman asking him what he was searching for, he said he searched after a sermon, which he thought his masterpiece, against vanity.   " Fie upon it, fie upon it ! " cries he, " why do I ever leave that sermon out of my pocket ?   I wish it was within five miles ; I would willingly fetch it to read it you."—The gentleman answered there was no need, for he was cured of the passion.   " And for that

very reason," quoth Adams, "I would read it, for I am
confident you would admire it : indeed, I have never
been a greater enemy to any passion than that silly one
of vanity."

This fine satirical stroke, which has often been com-
mented upon, really cuts with a double edge, for while
it is amusing enough that Adams should be vain enough
to walk ten miles merely that his companion should admire
his denunciation of vanity, it is perhaps even more entertaining that this little display, at which, we are told,
Wilson merely smiled, should come on top of the latter's
remark that vanity is the worst of passions. The fact
is, of course, that vanity is not the worst of passions, and
Wilson ought to have found food for thought in this
little incident and his attitude towards it, thought that
might have led him to reconsider his ethical system.
An equally entertaining scene is to be found in the eighth
chapter of the third book, a chapter that Fielding, very
characteristically, labels *Which some readers will think
too short, others too long.* Adams and his two young
friends have arrived at an ale-house, and after a rather
meagre supper of bread and cheese and ale, the parson
expressed great contempt for the folly of mankind, who
sacrificed their hopes of heaven to the acquisition of vast
wealth, since so much comfort was to be found in the
humblest state and the lowest provision. A fellow

traveller, a grave man, smoking his pipe by the fire, immediately agrees and begins an attack upon riches that arouses Adams to great enthusiasm. The two moralists then take turn and turn about denouncing the love of money and avowing their contempt for gold until a late hour. At last, the stranger, a priest of the Church of Rome in the dress of a layman, asks Adams to lend him eighteenpence to pay his reckoning. The good man promises to divide all the money he has about him, half a guinea, with his companion, but discovers, after some search, that his pocket has been picked and that he is now penniless :

"Bless me !" cried Adams. "I have certainly lost it ; I can never have spent it. Sir, as I am a Christian, I had a whole half-guinea in my pocket this morning, and have not now a single halfpenny of it left. Sure the devil must have taken it from me !"—"Sir," answered the priest, smiling, "you need make no excuses ; if you are not willing to lend me the money, I am contented."—"Sir," cries Adams, "if I had the greatest sum in the world—ay, if I had ten pounds about me— I would bestow it all to rescue any Christian from distress. I am more vexed at my loss on your account than my own. Was there ever anything so unlucky ? Because I have no money in my pocket, I shall be suspected to be no Christian. . . ."

After some further talk, the stranger decides to leave at once, and calling for the landlord, explains the position to him. The landlord, making the best of a bad business, agrees to let his reckoning stand as a loan, and the stranger quickly disappears into the night :

He was no sooner gone than the host fell a-shaking his head, and declared, if he had suspected the fellow had no money, he would not have drawn him a single drop of drink, saying he despaired of ever seeing his face again, for that he looked like a confounded rogue. " Rabbit the fellow," cries he, " I thought, by his talking so much about riches, that he had a hundred pounds at least in his pocket."

At this, we are told, Adams, equally penniless, reproached the speaker for suspicions that were not becoming a Christian, and then retired to bed and fell asleep without considering how his own interview with the landlord would fall out in the morning.

There is a capital scene that takes place on the very next day, a scene in which Adams shows himself to be a true friend and a good Christian but nevertheless a very tactless companion. Fanny has been kidnapped from the inn, and Joseph and Adams, after a tremendous struggle, have been tied to the bedposts. Joseph is in despair and loudly bewails the loss of his mistress. Adams, very sore and ruffled, sitting with his back to his companion because they have been tied that way, endeavours to comfort him, points out that it is the business of a

man and a Christian to summon Reason to his aid, and
so forth.   He goes on :

"Be comforted, therefore, child ; I say be comforted.
It is true you have lost the prettiest, kindest, loveliest,
sweetest young woman, one with whom you might have
expected to have lived in happiness, virtue, and innocence ;
by whom you might have promised yourself many little
darlings, who would have been the delight of your youth
and the comfort of your age.   You have not only lost
her, but have reason to fear the utmost violence which
lust and power can inflict upon her   Now, indeed, you
may easily raise ideas of horror."

Joseph, as well he might, breaks in upon this discourse
with a cry of despair ; but Adams bids him remember
that he is a Christian, that no accident happens to us
without the divine permission, and that it is the duty of
a man and a Christian to submit.   He then proceeds to
give reasons why we have no right to complain against
our destiny, and excellent reasons they are too.   But
when he has reached his " Thirdly " and is going forward
magnificently, poor Joseph, whom Fielding has suddenly
dowered with life, breaks in once more only to say what
poor stricken humanity has always said to the easy
philosopher whose relish for his dialectic has got the
upper hand of his dismay at the situation :

"Oh, sir ! " cried Joseph, "all this is very true, and
very fine, and I could hear you all day if I was not so

grieved at heart as now I am."—"Would you take physic," says Adams, "when you are well, and refuse it when you are sick? Is not comfort to be administered to the afflicted, and not to those who rejoice or those who are at ease?"—"Oh! you have not spoken one word of comfort to me yet!" returned Joseph.—"No!" cries Adams; "what am I then doing? what can I say to comfort you?"—"O tell me," cried Joseph, "that Fanny will escape back to my arms, that they shall again enclose that lovely creature, with all her sweetness, all her untainted innocence about her!"

In the end, Adams, by sheer force of character, does succeed in quieting his companion; but actually the latter's first cry is unanswerable except by a counter-cry, somewhat louder. There is the whole history of religions and philosophies in this little piece of dialogue.

Later in the story, in the parson's house, Joseph shows great impatience to be married because he feels that he will never have an easy moment till Fanny is absolutely his; and Adams takes it upon himself to rebuke the lover in measured terms for this impatience. He begins with a little dissertation on marriage and then goes on to attack fear as a want of confidence in that Power in which we should alone put our trust. Further, he points out, all passions are criminal in their excess, and even love itself, if it is not subservient to our duty, may render us blind to it. Feeling the pulpit stairs beneath his feet, he proceeds:

You are too much inclined to passion, child, and have set your affection so absolutely on this young woman, that, if God required her at your hands, I fear you would reluctantly part with her. Now, believe me, no Christian ought so to set his heart on any person or thing in this world, but that, whenever it shall be required or taken from him in any manner by Divine Providence, he may be able peaceably, quietly, and contentedly to resign it."

Unfortunately for the success of this homily, at this very moment a person rushes into the room to inform Adams that his youngest son is drowned. In a flash, the easy moralist has disappeared and the parent has taken his place :

He stood silent a moment, and soon began to stamp about the room and deplore his loss with the bitterest agony.

The rôles are now reversed.

Joseph, who was overwhelmed with concern likewise, recovered himself sufficiently to endeavour to comfort the parson ; in which attempt he used many arguments that he had at several times remembered out of his own discourses, both in private and public (for he was a great enemy to the passions, and preached nothing more than the conquest of them by reason and grace), but he was not at leisure now to hearken to his advice. "Child, child," said he, "do not go about impossibilities. Had it been any other of my children, I could have borne it with patience ; but my little prattler, the darling and comfort of my old age,—the little wretch, to be snatched out of life just at his entrance into it ; the sweetest, best-tempered boy, who never did a thing to offend me. . . ."

The good man is now inconsolable and dwells pitifully on the virtues of his lost child. A few minutes later, however, the boy himself appears, wet through, for though he had indeed fallen into the water, he had been rescued by a certain pedlar. The joy of Adams, we are told, is now as extravagant as his grief had been ; he kisses the boy a thousand times and dances about the room in an ecstasy of relief. Unfortunately, when all the rejoicing is at an end, he sees fit to resume the part of moralist and adviser, and actually begins once more to tell Joseph that he must not give way too much to his passions if he wishes to be happy. This is too much, even for the faithful Joseph, who points out that it is easier to give advice than to act upon it. At this, Adams, in danger of losing his authority, replies that Joseph is ignorant of the tenderness of fatherly affection, that the loss of a child is one of those great trials where our grief may be allowed to become immoderate ; and when Joseph counters by declaring that the loss of a well-beloved mistress may equal that of a well-beloved child, Adams, driven into a corner, strikes out boldly :

" Yes, but such love (of a wife) is foolishness and wrong in itself, and ought to be conquered," answered Adams ; " it savours too much of the flesh."—" Sure, sir," says

Joseph, " it is not sinful to love my wife, no, not even to doat on her to distraction ! "—" Indeed but it is," says Adams. " Every man ought to love his wife, no doubt ; we are commanded to do so ; but we ought to love her with moderation and discretion."—" I am afraid I shall be guilty of some sin in spite of all my endeavours," says Joseph ; " for I shall love without any moderation, I am sure."—" You talk foolishly and childishly," cried Adams. . . .

And now all would be well, only that man has a tangle of relationships, and Adams in playing the father and the mentor has forgotten that he is also a husband and that his good lady is present :

" Indeed," says Mrs. Adams, who had listened to the latter part of their conversation, " you talk more foolishly yourself. I hope, my dear, you will never preach any such doctrines as that husbands can love their wives too well. If I knew you had such a sermon in the house, I am sure I would burn it ; and I declare, if I had not been convinced you had loved me as well as you could, I can answer for myself, I should have hated and despised you. Marry come up ! Fine doctrine indeed ! A wife hath a right to insist on her husband's loving her as much as ever he can ; and he is a sinful villain who doth not. Doth he not promise to love her, and to comfort her, and to cherish her, and all that ? I am sure I remember it all as well as if I had repeated it over but yesterday, and shall never forget it. Besides, I am certain you do not preach as you practise ; for you have been a loving and cherishing husband to me. that 's the truth on 't ; and why you should endeavour to put such wicked nonsense into this young man's head I cannot devise. . . ."

We shall do well to let the lady (who has not finished yet) have the last word ; and take our leave of our friend Adams, and his old wig, his nightcap and torn cassock, his Aeschylus, his bleak ethics and his brave, warm heart, standing like many another philosopher before an indignant woman with his fine theories crashing about him. " I am certain you do not preach as you practise " : she has said the last word ; he, almost alone of these characters, preaches well but practises even better ; and " the parsons who preached last Sunday " will have done well if they have done half the good that brave old Adams, sitting bewildered in a ditch or fighting in an inn-parlour, has contrived to do amidst the laughter of six generations.

THE BROTHERS SHANDY

THOUGH it would be difficult to commend My Uncle Toby either too often or too heartily, nevertheless some of the praise he has received might, in all justice, have been diverted to his neglected brother Walter. The bright regimentals have caught many an eye that has allowed the domestic philosopher, in his old wig and dusty coat, to pass unremarked. Toby, it is true, is set against the better background ; he it is who brings us to the campaigns in Flanders, to the more amiable and diverting warfare on the bowling-green, and to the last and, we fear, most faint-hearted siege of all, that of the Widow Wadman ; whereas Mr. Shandy, with his more abstruse concerns, only leads us to Slawkenbergius on Noses and other choke-pears. Toby appeals to the eye ; we can see him, parading for the Wadman campaign, in his great ramallie-wig, tarnished gold-laced hat and huge cockade of flimsy taffeta, in his blue and gold coat (that "had become so miserably too strait for him") and red plush breeches ; he cuts a fine figure in the imagination, limping past to the widow's or conducting

128

one of his dream-sieges from the sentry-box or puffing
at his pipe, his red beaming foolish face all aglow, at his
brother's fireside.   Such little pictures do not easily
fade out of the memory, and Toby lives on for us long
after we have closed and put away the volume that
contains him, so that at will we can recapture his acquaintance and never find it more than a step or so to his
bowling-green and mimic battlements.   In his simplicity,
kindness, and innocent enthusiasm, in his warm humanity,
he is a more lovable figure than his brother ; Sterne sees
to it that we shall fall in love with him, and, indeed, sometimes goes too far in sentiment, dropping too much
sugar in Toby's pot.   There is, for example, that famous
anecdote about Toby and the fly :

—Go—says he, one day at dinner, to an overgrown
one which had buzzed about his nose, and tormented
him cruelly all dinner-time,—and which after infinite
attempts, he had caught at last, as it flew by him ;—I 'll
not hurt thee, says my uncle Toby, rising from his chair,
and going across the room, with the fly in his hand,—
I 'll not hurt a hair of thy head :—Go, says he, lifting
up the sash, and opening his hand as he spoke, to let it
escape ;—go, poor devil, get thee gone, why should I
hurt thee ?—This world surely is wide enough to hold
both thee and me.

which has been admired times without number, and by
some very good judges.   Even Coleridge, who has some

very brilliant critical passages on Sterne buried away among his notes and fragments of lectures, calls it a " beautiful passage." But while the incident is very artfully related, it is catch-penny, with an appeal that is too gross ; we can see Sterne bowing and smirking in the background and then passing round the hat into which we are asked to drop a tear of sensibility. Nevertheless, in spite of such doses of sweet melted butter, Toby remains the more lovable of the two. Yet as a comic figure his more irascible brother is equally successful. Side by side, on their own hearth, there is nothing to choose between them, and indeed it is the conjunction and the contrast that are so piquant. The Shandy family, with its several retainers, Trim, Obadiah, Susannah, with Dr. Slop and Yorick in attendance, is best enjoyed as a group, in which each figure stands out in exquisite relief.

The head of the family, Mr. Walter Shandy (My Father), we are told, was originally a Turkey merchant, but when the story opens he has left off business and has retired to his family estate in the country. He is extremely regular in matters both of business and pleasure (and no one who has ever read the opening chapters of *Tristram Shandy* is likely to forget the fact), somewhat short-tempered and rough-tongued, but at heart very kind and generous. Like many retired men of business, both in that century and this, having made his fortune by using

his common-sense, having depended for so many years
upon the fact that two and two make four, he has now
given common-sense a holiday and passes his time trying
to discover if two and two will possibly make five. He
is that very familiar eighteenth-century figure, the
amateur philosopher, a collector of the antiques and
curios of intellectual theory, a connoisseur of finely spun
dialectic and debate. He has reached the stage that
most men with brains arrive at during their third year
at the university, the stage of the prize essay paradox,
when far-fetched and elaborate theories are inevitably
preferred to simple ones, when the more subtle reasoning
is always the more acceptable, when nothing is simplified
except the few things in this life that never should be
simplified. The mind, delighted with its discovery
that it can move at all, jumps and skips about all day :
the intellect sows its wild oats. Most intelligent men
pass through this stage at some time or other, usually
early in life, but some, like Samuel Butler, another retired
man of affairs, arrive at it late and then never leave it ;
they are brilliant undergraduates for the rest of their
days. Mr. Shandy, who is not unlike Butler, except
that his devotion to ideas is perhaps more selfless than
Butler's was, is really a brilliant third-year man and should
be writing prize essays instead of trying, with a notable
lack of success, to lure his incurious family into debate.

Having fallen into this state of mind rather late in life,
he is in full possession of all the symptoms.   Sterne knew
what he was about when he made Mr. Shandy a retired
merchant, for many years of money-making are apt to
leave a man intellectually innocent, so that when he quits
his counting-house for the last time he is just as likely
to make the delightful discovery that there are such things
as paradoxes in the world as he is to reveal to himself the
charms of gardening.   At this very moment, buried
away in snug and bookish villas, there are probably a
few score Mr. Shandies, bent on proving that a gravel
soil is necessary to produce great genius, that all our
political progress is the work of the ten lost tribes, that
the Arabs first invented sin, that the world will not be
saved until all the red-haired have vanished from its
surface.   Such persons are not scholars, even in their
retirement, but they contrive to amass a great quantity
of odd scraps of learning, they come to their books, which
are for the most part curious out-of-the-way volumes,
with a certain freshness and innocence and so tend
to believe in them whole-heartedly.   Tristram Shandy,
wishing to emphasise his father's native gifts as an
orator and dialectician, seems to underestimate Mr.
Shandy's learning, for he remarks :

And yet, 'tis strange, he had never read Cicero, nor
Quintilian *de Oratore*, nor Isocrates, nor Aristotle, nor

Longinus amongst the ancients ;—nor Vossius, nor
Scioppius, nor Ramus, nor Farnaby amongst the moderns ;
—and what is more astonishing, he had never in his
whole life the least light or spark of subtlety struck into
his mind, by one single lecture upon Crackenthorpe or
Burgersdicius, or any Dutch logician or commentator ;
—he knew not so much as in what the difference of an
argument *ad ignorantiam* and an argument *ad hominem*
consisted ; so that I well remember, when he went up
along with me to enter my name at Jesus College in . . .
—it was a matter of just wonder with my worthy tutor,
and two or three fellows of that learned society,—that
a man who knew not so much as the names of his
tools, should be able to work after that fashion with
them.

Mr. Shandy has more learning than one would gather
from this passage, for he bolsters up his odd theories with
a multitude of instances and examples. Moreover, we
are told that he once wrote a Life of Socrates. The
Shandean system is the familiar one of intellectual crankish-
ness, which holds that the fate of humanity depends upon
its taking some curious little step, such as contriving that
children shall be born into the world feet first ; which
believes that its own particular crotchet, such as Mr.
Shandy's "magic bias of Christian names," will save the
world. The amateur scientists and philosophers of
the eighteenth century undoubtedly did their share of
crotcheteering and were never at a loss for a panacea, but

they were a mere handful when compared with their descendants, the crotcheteers of our time, which is the very age that Mr. Shandy should have chosen to live in. With us, I have no doubt, he would have been completely happy. But he is at Shandy Hall, with his wife and brother Toby for company, and he has trials even beyond the lot of most philosophers.

The greatest of his trials arises from the fact that he is a philosopher, a logician, an orator, without an audience. Small wonder that he is so irritable, for never was a born debater so unfortunately placed. His wife and his brother are entirely devoid of intellectual curiosity. He has, as Coleridge pointed out, " a craving for sympathy in exact proportion to the oddity and unsympathisability of what he proposes," his oddest theories, like lame children, being the dearest to him ; and further, like so many of us, he does not desire either total and final disagreement or immediate acquiescence on the part of his audience ; he wishes to be disagreed with at first so that he may have some opportunity of displaying his powers of debate and persuasion, which will in the end inevitably bring his audience into agreement with him. Tristram, after presenting us with that delightful specimen of the argument *ad hominem* of his father's on the subject of names (" Your son,—your dear son,—from whose sweet and open temper you have so much to expect.—Your Billy,

Sir !—would you, for the world, have called him Judas ? "),
remarks :

But, indeed, to speak of my father as he was ; he was
certainly irresistible ; both in his orations and disputations ;
—he was born an orator ;—θεοδιδακτός. Persuasion
hung upon his lips, and the elements of Logic and Rhetoric
were so blended up in him,—and, withal, he had so shrewd
a guess at the weaknesses and passions of his respondent,—
that Nature might have stood up and said,—" This man
is eloquent."—In short, whether he was on the weak
or the strong side of the question, 'twas hazardous in
either case to attack him.

But such talkers, whose powers of persuasion dance
attendance upon their vanity, do not merely want to
drive certain conclusions into their listeners' heads ;
they are not bagmen or politicians, they are artists, whose
fantastic theories only increase the difficulty and delight
of their elaborate justifications and defences, and like
all artists, unless they have a public worthy of their art,
they are nothing. Mr. Shandy's irritation is not, on the
whole, due to the fact that he cannot gain his point and
compel submission to his crotchets, but is the result of
his knowledge that all the subtle reasoning, all the tricks
of debate, by means of which he could, in more know-
ledgeable company, win assent to his most ridiculous
theories, are wasted on his audience. And as these
theories have for the most part been chosen to demonstrate

his skill, being difficult to prove, he has all the more reason to be annoyed that such skill should be thrown away : he is like a perspiring juggler before a company of the blind.   His naïve intellectual vanity, the mark of his kind everywhere, remains unsatisfied.

It is hard to determine, from his point of view, which is the more unsatisfactory listener, his wife or his brother. Mrs. Shandy, that excellent woman, has not an idea in her head ; she has a few convictions, which she does not allow any argument to disturb, but for the rest, like a good wife, she is ready to agree with anything her strange husband may say, so that either he meets with stubborn opposition that no amount of talk can break down, or he meets with immediate and uncomprehending ac-. quiescence.   When it is a practical question, such as the employment of Dr. Slop in place of the usual old midwife, a step that Mr. Shandy is prepared to defend with the utmost subtlety, she is simply not to be moved :

Amongst the many and excellent reasons, with which my father had urged my mother to accept of Dr. Slop's assistance preferably to that of the old woman,—there was one of a very singular nature ; which, when he had done arguing the matter with her as a Christian, and came to argue it over again with her as a philosopher, he had put his whole strength to, depending indeed upon it as his sheet-anchor.——It failed him ; tho' from no defect in the argument itself ; but that, do what he could, he was not able for his soul to make her comprehend the drift of it.—Cursed luck !—said he to himself, one afternoon, as he walked out of the room, after he had been stating it for an hour and a half to her, to no manner of purpose ;—cursed luck !—said he, biting his lips as he shut the door,—for a man to be master of one of the finest chains of reasoning in nature,—and have a wife at the same time with such a headpiece, that he cannot hang up a single inference within side of it, to save his soul from destruction. . . .

When other matters, of less immediate concern to herself, are discussed, she simply hastens to agree and so deprives her husband of that mimic warfare in which he delights. There never was a human being with less intellectual curiosity :

It was a consuming vexation to my father, that my mother never asked the meaning of a thing she did not understand.

—That she is not a woman of science, my father would say—is her misfortune—but she might ask a question.—

My mother never did.—In short, she went out of the world at last without knowing whether it turned round, or stood still.—My father had officiously told her above a thousand times which way it was,—but she always forgot.

For these reasons, a discourse seldom went on much further betwixt them, than a proposition,—a reply, and a rejoinder ; at the end of which, it generally took breath for a few minutes (as in the affair of the breeches), and then went on again. . . .

Certainly that curtain dialogue on the subject of Tristram's breeching shows Mrs. Shandy to be not merely an unphilosophical hearer but one of those very amiable but irritating conversationalists who are nothing more than echoes.   No doubt there are husbands who would regard such extreme complaisance on the part of a wife with something like envy, but actually one does not need to be a Mr. Shandy to find it particularly annoying, dealing sudden death to all conversation :

We should begin, said my father, turning himself half round in bed, and shifting his pillow a little towards my mother's, as he opened the debate.—We should begin to think, Mrs. Shandy, of putting this boy into breeches.—

We should so,—said my mother.—We defer it, my dear, quoth my father, shamefully.—

I think we do, Mr. Shandy,—said my mother.

—Not but the child looks extremely well, said my father, in his vests and tunics.—

—He does look very well in them,—replied my mother.—

And for that reason it would be almost a sin, added my father, to take him out of 'em.—

—It would be so,—said my mother :—But indeed he is growing a very tall lad,—rejoined my father.

—He is very tall for his age, indeed, said my mother.—

—I can not (making two syllables of it) imagine, quoth my father,—who the deuce he takes after.—

I cannot conceive, for my life,—said my mother.—

Humph !—said my father. . . .

and so on to the end of the chapter. In this dialogue, and indeed in all the passages of talk between Mr. and Mrs. Shandy, there is a closeness and an economy under the apparent carelessness of the writer, who contrives to bring forward (as Coleridge noted) " those minutiae of thought and feeling which appear trifles, yet have an importance for the moment " with the minimum expenditure of words, that give a new turn to narration and begin a new chapter in the history of the English novel.

But Mr. Shandy is no better off with his brother Toby as an audience. Toby is not entirely barren of ideas, but he has no more intellectual curiosity than Mrs. Shandy, and he is probably still more irritating because he has a trick of showing some gleam of interest in his brother's speculations and then, when the latter, delighted at such interest, warms to his work, of suddenly blotting out this gleam, promptly shutting off, as it were, his curiosity ; so that by the time Mr. Shandy is at the height of his peroration, Toby's mind is once more a blank and he is quietly whistling *Lillabullero*. Poor Mr. Shandy has been led within sight of the Promised Land only to be whisked away again into the wilderness. That was a great moment for our philosopher when, after the arrival of Dr. Slop and Obadiah, he and Toby had waited downstairs for what seemed to them an age

but what was actually two hours and ten minutes.   Mr.
Shandy, hoping against hope that there might be here
an opportunity for " a metaphysical dissertation upon the
subject of duration and its simple modes," remarked :
" I know not how it happens, but it seems an age."   He
knew very well how it happened and was determined
that Toby should share his knowledge.   But Toby, for
once, displayed an interest that should have pleased him,
but actually did nothing of the kind because it looked as
if it would rob him of any chance of explaining the
matter :

—'Tis owing entirely, quoth my uncle Toby, to the
succession of our ideas.

My father, who had an itch, in common with all
philosophers, of reasoning upon everything which
happened, and accounting for it too—proposed infinite
pleasure to himself in this, of the succession of ideas, and
had not the least apprehension of having it snatched out
of his hands by my uncle Toby, who (honest man !)
generally took every thing as it happened ;—and who,
of all things in the world, troubled his brain least with
abstruse thinking ;—the ideas of time and space—or
how we came by those ideas—or of what stuff they were
made—or whether they were born with us—or we
picked them up afterwards as we went along—or
whether we did it in frocks—or not till we had got into
breeches—with a thousand other inquiries and disputes
about Infinity, Prescience, Liberty, Necessity, and so
forth, upon whose desperate and unconquerable theories

so many fine heads have been turned and cracked—never did my uncle Toby's the least injury at all ; my father knew it—and was no less surprised than he was disappointed, with my uncle's fortuitous solution.

Do you understand the theory of that affair ? replied my father.

Not I, quoth my uncle.

—But you have some ideas, said my father, of what you talk about ?—

No more than my horse, replied my uncle Toby.

And then all Mr. Shandy's attempts to explain come to nothing in face of this cheerful ignorance ; Toby remains quietly impervious to ideas, and only expresses his bewilderment and indifference until his brother happens, unluckily for him, to mention "a regular succession of ideas of one sort and another, which follow each other in train just like——" Then Toby, preparing to mount his hobby-horse, his mind aroused at last, cuts in with "A train of artillery," and is promptly snubbed for his pains. It is unfortunate for Mr. Shandy's oratory that Toby takes everything literally and relates all he hears to his own experience, chiefly military, so that either it means nothing and leaves him blankly puffing his pipe or whistling, or it starts a train of thought of his own, which he never fails to pursue. There is a memorable little chapter that records how Mr. Shandy, after flinging himself down on his bed in despair at the news that

Tristram's nose had been crushed by Dr. Slop (long noses being one of Mr. Shandy's crotchets, as the reader learns to his cost), has the misfortune to voice that despair metaphorically to Toby :

Did ever man, brother Toby, cried my father, raising himself upon his elbow, and turning himself round to the opposite side of the bed, where my uncle Toby was sitting in his old fringed chair, with his chin resting upon his crutch—did ever a poor unfortunate man, brother Toby, cried my father, receive so many lashes ?

—The most I ever saw given, quoth my uncle Toby (ringing the bell at the bed's head for Trim), was to a grenadier, I think in Mackay's regiment.

—Had my uncle Toby shot a bullet through my father's heart, he could not have fallen down with his nose upon the quilt more suddenly.

Bless me ! said my uncle Toby. . .

There is perhaps nothing richer in the whole book than the scene that follows, in which Trim appears and talks of his brother Tom, who was tortured upon the rack for nothing but marrying a Jew's widow who sold sausages ; and Uncle Toby rewards his corporal with a pension for his long service and goodness of heart ; and Mr. Shandy, in a Socratic posture, holding fast his forefinger between his finger and thumb, discourses on Man and his Destiny with Toby, seated in his old fringed chair, valanced around with parti-coloured worsted bobs ; and the two lovable creatures go downstairs, discussing the name Trismegistus, and Toby catches Mr. Shandy on the shinbone with his crutch and Mr. Shandy forgets his pain in the double success of his repartees ; and they arrive at the bottom in time to ask Susannah how her mistress does, and are snubbed, and shake their heads together, the married man remarking how all the women in a household give themselves airs when the mistress is brought to bed, the bachelor pointing out that " 'Tis we who sink an inch lower.—If I meet but a woman with child—I do it." And so the scepticism and restless intellectual vanity of the one, and the innocence and simple faith of the other, in the face of these mysteries of birth and sex and death, run together and forget their differences in a concerted head-shaking.

It surprises no one to learn that a great many of Mr. Shandy's intellectual whimsies were borrowed by Sterne from Burton and other old authors. Mr. Shandy was quite capable of filching them himself. On the other hand, we have to make a distinct effort to realise that a number of Uncle Toby's most characteristic remarks are also plagiarisms. Thus, when Mr. Shandy is worrying himself and his brother on the subject of " the various accounts which learned men of different kinds of knowledge have given the world of the causes of the short and long noses," and Toby replies : " There is no cause but one why one man's nose is longer than another's, but

because God pleases to have it so "; this is not only
Grangousier's solution, as Mr. Shandy points out, but
his identical remark. And yet, so strong is the spell
of Sterne's characterisation, all these things are to us
Toby's own, falling from his lips as naturally as the " Good
morning " fell from ours at breakfast time. Everything
he says and does is in character, and when we have met
him once or twice, not all the plagiarism in the world
could viscerate him or even steal a breath from his rich
individuality. Mr. Shandy is an equally triumphant
creation, but he is not presented in the same way that
Toby is and is hardly so firmly seated, as a figure, in our
imagination ; we know how he thinks and talks, but
for the rest, he is somewhat shadowy and not easily called
to mind. Toby is as solid and unmistakable as a hill.
At any moment, we can see him in his faded regimentals,
with his lame leg and crutch, very complacently smoking
his pipe by the fire. Though we are given much less
of his talk than of Mr. Shandy's, we know more about
him ; we know how he was wounded during the siege
of Namur, how he retired on half-pay, attended by
Corporal Trim, to a small house near Shandy Hall, how
he first mounted his hobby-horse, his enthusiasm for
fortifications and sieges, and how it ran away with him.
He is more concretely presented, and has also a larger
background, so that he soon becomes a more familiar

personage than his brother. As we have seen, he is the simplest of mortals, and, indeed, one step further along the path of simplicity and he would be tumbling into idiocy. As it is, he is only saved by his manliness and faith. He has known terrible things, and was among the cannon when his brother, bold in speculation, was among his ledgers, but his innocent faith in God and his fellow-men has never been shaken, and now that he is in retirement, now that he has known the worst and left it behind, his faith never will be shaken. We cannot appreciate him to the full unless we see him against his background, and remember that, in his time, he has been as bold in face of the enemy as his brother, with his odd theories, is now in face of common-sense and the arguments of opposing theorists. Just as Sterne knew what he was about when he made Mr. Shandy a retired merchant, so too he made no mistake when he made this unsophisticated, kindly, generous, childlike soul, Uncle Toby, a retired army officer. The army has sent out into the civilian world a host of Uncle Tobies (bating a few eccentricities), men who have known bloodshed and horror and yet are as simple as children. Nor is this very surprising. A soldier's life is a sheltered life, more so, in some respects, than that of many a maiden lady living in retirement at a watering-place. It shuts a man off from all manner of problems and temptations, frees him from so many snares, closes so many paths to dishonour ; and yet it asks, in return, for nothing more than the observance of a few simple loyalties. It demands obedience and courage and tends to foster the spirit of happy comradeship ; it keeps alive the boy in a man and protects him against a thousand meannesses. A soldier is frequently a child who has seen some of the most terrible sights the world has to show, and yet remains a child ; and it is probably this curious combination of strength, courage, and innocence that has made the soldier irresistible in love, for no combination of qualities in a man could be more attractive to the average woman.

Sterne had not spent his earliest years wandering from camp to camp for nothing : he knew his men. Both Toby and Corporal Trim, though they are both strongly individualised characters, are typical retired soldiers. They have few ideas and a very narrow range of interests but have a fund of reminiscence. Having served in the same company, they have a kind of common stock of memories, and Trim not only attends Toby as valet, groom, barber, cook, sempster, and nurse, he also serves as a memory, to which Toby can appeal when in doubt. "Was it Mackay's regiment, quoth my uncle, where the poor grenadier was so unmercifully whipped at Bruges about the ducats ?—O Christ !—he was innocent ! cried Trim, with a deep sigh.—And he was whipped,

may it please your honour, almost to death's door.—They
had better have shot him outright, as he begged, and he
had gone directly to heaven, for he was as innocent as
your honour.—I thank thee, Trim, quoth my uncle
Toby." Literature is filled with old soldiers, but there
is nothing better than this Trim. . He has that curious
sententiousness, that punctiliousness, that love of unnecessary detail in his recitals, that curious mixture of
servility and impudence, under which there is a genuine,
even intense devotion, which mark the type anywhere
and everywhere. He is always on hand, and in spite of
his seeming deference, his " may it please your honour,"
his " by your leave," he cannot be prevented from
breaking into the conversation ; and as he has an even
more literal mind than his master, his interventions
produce some ludicrous results. He it was who, when
Mr. Shandy was discussing the teaching of grammar
and, in particular, the use of the auxiliaries, pointed out
that " The Danes, an' please your honour, who were
on the left at the siege of Limerick, were all auxiliaries."
But he is a very useful fellow, and worth a few liberties,
for there is nothing he cannot do, from collecting the
material for a miniature siege to devising a campaign
against the heart of a widow. Nothing could be more
pleasant than the sight of these two simple, battered
warriors, master and man, when they are together.

Each would be lost without the other.   Their memories, coming together, strike fire from one another :

—For my own part, Trim, though I can see little or no difference betwixt my nephew's being called Tristram or Trismegistus—yet as the thing sits so near my brother's heart, Trim—I would freely have given a hundred pounds rather than that it should have happened.—A hundred pounds, an' please your honour ! replied Trim, —I would not give a cherry-stone to boot.—Nor would I, Trim, upon my own account, quoth my uncle Toby— but my brother, whom there is no arguing with in this case —maintains that a great deal more depends, Trim, upon Christian names, than what ignorant people imagine— for he says there never was a great or heroic action performed since the world began by one called Tristram— nay, he will have it, Trim, that a man can neither be learned, or wise, or brave.—'Tis all fancy, an' please your honour—I fought just as well, replied the corporal, when the regiment called me Trim, as when they called me James Butler.—And for my own part, said my uncle Toby, though I should blush to boast of myself, Trim —yet had my name been Alexander, I could have done no more at Namur than my duty.—Bless your honour ! cried Trim, advancing three steps as he spoke, does a man think of his Christian name when he goes upon the attack ?—Or when he stands in the trench, Trim ? cried my uncle Toby, looking firm.—Or when he enters a breach ? said Trim, pushing in between two chairs.— Or forces the lines ? cried my uncle, rising up, and pushing his crutch like a pike.—Or facing a platoon ? cried Trim, presenting his stick like a firelock.—Or when he marches up the glacis ? cried my uncle Toby, looking warm and setting his foot upon his stool.——

Toby is naïvely proud of Trim's accomplishments (" He can read it, quoth my uncle Toby, as well as I can.—— Trim, I assure you, was the best scholar in my company, and should have had the next halberd, but for the poor fellow's misfortune "), and is always ready to show him off to the company, Trim himself being by no means unwilling, whether it is matter of reading a sermon, going through the catechism, or doing his drill. Both Trim and his master, taken together, are at their best in that story of Le Fever, when the very sight of these two brave old simpletons, conspiring together to do good, though it could not save their fellow soldier, is a tonic to the reader

Toby belongs to a class of characters made up of people who, strictly considered, can be set apart from the ordinary comic personages ; they are lovable characters, who steal our affections as children steal them, and at whose vagaries and innocent preoccupations we smile just as we smile at those of children. It is more than likely that there is something of the child in all the comic figures that are not merely satirical sketches. Even in Falstaff, who, to speak truly, is little better than one of the wicked, there is a child, greedy for sensation, clamouring for notice, a thoughtless, incorrigible, adorable child,

hidden away somewhere, and it is this child we are willing
to indulge, and it is for his sake that we forgive the old
ruffian in whose heart he still lives on, forgive him so
much and so often.   But in Uncle Toby, and in all the
figures that his influence has probably called into existence,
the child predominates.   We never lose sight of him,
prancing on his hobby-horse.   Sterne makes such great
play with this hobby-horse that it is almost impossible to
think of Toby apart from his fortifications and sieges.
We are told, with a wealth of crafty detail, how it all
began when Toby was still laid up with his wound, and
how, with Trim's invaluable assistance, a bookish interest
was gradually transformed into a glorious game.   If
there is any reader who is unfortunate enough to be
unacquainted with Toby's hobby, he must be satisfied
in this place with the briefest description.   Toby and
Trim took the plan of any fortified town invested by
Marlborough and the Allies, enlarged it upon a scale to
the exact size of the bowling-green, and then, by means
of pack-thread and piquets driven into the earth, trans-
ferred the lines from the paper to the ground.   Toby
would then determine " the depths and slopes of the
ditches,—the talus of the glacis, and the precise height
of the several banquets, parapets, etc.," and set Trim
to work upon constructing the miniature fortification.
This done, the two enthusiasts, following the latest news

from the front, would solemnly invest the place and conduct the siege, step by step, with the Allies. By what astonishing shifts and devices, such as the use of mutilated jack-boots and two Turkish pipes, the bowling-green was gradually brought nearer and nearer to the likeness of a battlefield, there is no space here to tell; the reader must learn these things for himself and they will repay his study. It is sufficient to say that both master and man are whole-hearted in their devotion to this unusual pastime, that nothing is spared (not even the window cords in Mr. Shandy's house, as Tristram learned to his cost when the window came crashing down at a very awkward moment) if it will serve the besiegers, that their thoughts never stray very far away from their fortifications. Never were there such enthusiasts.

It is an old trick to make your comic figure the victim of a ruling passion, a man of one idea, with a mind like a jack-in-the-box, responding only when a certain spring is touched, a creature somewhere half-way between reason and unreason, at once mad enough and sane enough to be a fit target for laughter. The more ridiculous his ruling passion happens to be, the more ridiculous he himself becomes. Such figures, with their catchwords and mechanical gestures, too unreasonable to be taken seriously and not mad enough to be pitied or feared,

have always been part of the humorist's stock-in-trade ;
there is always one of these personages on hand when
the occasion demands a little comic relief.   They neither
ask for nor obtain our sympathy ;   they perform their
tricks, and after being given a round of contemptuous
laughter, they are hurried off the scene and out of our
imagination.   At their best, they belong to satirical
literature.   But while Toby has a ruling passion (if
ever a man had), there is a gulf between him and the type
of character we have just noticed.   Sterne realised that
once you have made a character lovable, his devotion to
some absurdity or other can still be amusing in the old
way, but something new has been added.   Now that we
are in sympathy with him, and probably regard him with
affection, we can take pleasure in his pleasure ;   something of his excitement and delight is communicated to
us ;   no longer are we entirely detached, coldly watching
him making a fool of himself, for he is beginning to make
a fool of us, a happy fool, like himself.   We are still a
little detached, can still laugh at him because he is so
hobby-ridden and one-idea'd, but something sympathetic,
friendly, affectionate is burgeoning in our amusement.
Just as happy lovers and friends always laugh at one
another because, in some odd fashion, they have discovered
the innocence and childishness of each other, so too it
is the child in our comic figure that we have stumbled

upon, and we watch him mounting his hobby-horse as we watch a child at play. Bless him, he shall have his sieges and fortifications ! There never was a story or drama in which every man (including the author) was more " in his humour " than he is in *Tristram Shandy*, and yet we are worlds away from Jonson and the older satirical humorists. Sterne took good care to make Uncle Toby lovable first and eccentric afterwards, so that we follow his every movement with interest and affection. When Trim discovers that the bowling-green will make an excellent setting for mimic warfare, or that jack-boots, cut down, will serve as tolerable siege guns, and Toby is delighted, then we too, while we are laughing at them for being a pair of great children, are also delighted in our heart of hearts and would add a half-crown or so to Toby's guinea if we could only reach out to the hand of the ingenious Trim. The delight of the enthusiast is infectious, and nothing warms the heart more than the spectacle, so rare in recent fiction, of innocent pleasure, the romping and posturing, the absurdities and sudden splendours of that gleeful child which the passage of time and all the world's terrors and cruelties do not always succeed in killing. Fortunately too, though perhaps it was cunning rather than luck on Sterne's part, it happens that this absorbing pastime of Toby's has something childlike in its very composition, for what is it but a happy make-believe, an attempt to mimic, on a tiny scale, something that in itself is far removed from play, colossal, terrible, what is it but a rather more ingenious and adult affair of toy forts and tin soldiers ? It happens too that Sterne has made Uncle Toby the most, perhaps the only, sexually modest person in the book. Being Sterne, of course, he has to use this modesty as the spring-board for half a hundred plunges into rather tiresome, sniggering innuendo ; nevertheless, he did well to make Toby modest, both from his point of view and ours (the more we study this "dull fellow"—as Goldsmith, most unluckily, called him—the more we appreciate his infinite adroitness), if only because it would be difficult for a Captain Toby Shandy who was well versed and curious in love to enter our imagination as a great lovable child. The bloom would be gone ; and Toby, robbed of the bloom and flush of the innocent child in him, would not have successfully besieged so many hearts and have with-stood so long the saps and mines and assaulting regiments of Time.

For the benefits of the ordinary reader and not the student of literary curiosities, there is no novel of the first or even second rank that stands more in need of careful editing (not Bowdlerising) than this *Tristram Shandy*. The occasional indecencies in the narrative proper are apt to prove somewhat tiresome, particularly because their success depends not on the reader's frank acceptance of the facts of our physical life but on his (and more often her) half-shocked, half-delighted prudery ; but it is not the indecencies that prevent the work from making its widest appeal and that are therefore ready for pruning ; it is the tedious by-play, the wearisome digressions, the pseudo-learning, which drive us out of the company of the Shandy family and give us little or nothing in return for our exile, that should be ruthlessly cut out in any edition intended for the casual reader. These useless chapters clog the reader's progress through the narrative, and, unless he happens to be both imaginative and patient, they stand in the way of his appreciating the Shandy family, particularly its humours as a group, as it was meant to be appreciated. As a group, it is conceived and presented with exquisite tact. There is a perfect balance between satire and sentiment. We have already noticed how the Shandies, as we may call them, are at odds and cross-purposes intellectually ; a conversation can go forward among them without any single person in it understanding, or having the least desire to understand, what the other persons are talking about ; each follows his own nose and takes care that his mind keeps all its doors and windows closed. Such a notable want of intellectual sympathy and understanding, such a slavish devotion, on every hand, to a certain fixed set of ideas, such a rigid determination to shut out all thought that appears in a new form, deal death to philosophies and sciences and all reasonable intercourse and call up a horrible vision of humanity as a set of puppets worked on the wires of a few instincts. A satirist, loathing his species, could have taken such tragi-comical little creatures, each in the separate mechanical box of his mind, and made out of them a scene or narrative that would have jangled the nerves of a dozen generations. Sterne, however, having shown us this want of even the most ordinary intellectual sympathy, preserves the balance by emphasising what we might call the emotional kinship of his people. If the Shandies cannot share one another's thoughts, they can share one another's feelings. Any little crisis finds them, so to speak, in one another's arms, and produces a fine crop of tears and handshakes and " God bless you's." In short, their hearts are in the right place. Even we, who are content with fewer tears and hand-shakings, would be rather taken aback at the bleak satire of the narrative, when carefully considered, if the unity in feeling, the mutual trust and affection, of the Shandies were not so broadly and so often emphasised. It says something for the relative importance of wits, which are always at cross-purposes in this narrative, and hearts, which never fail to beat in unison here, that we carry away from Shandy Hall a picture of human happiness, and so gradually realise that these odd lovable creatures, the prancing philosopher, the simple Captain, and the rest, for all their bickering and their whimsies, have somehow stumbled upon the secret of the happy life.

MR. COLLINS

JANE AUSTEN only once achieved poetry, and that was when, in her early days, she created Mr. Collins. To many readers, particularly those who prefer the later Jane to the earlier, Mr. Collins is merely one figure in a notable gallery of comic figures, Mr. and Mrs. Bennet, Sir Walter Elliot, Mrs. Norris, Mr. Woodhouse, Miss Bates ; he falls into his place in this delicious company, and there is no more to be said about him. But he has always seemed to me an Austen character who stood by himself, a creature of larger stature than the rest, or one who is presented to us, shall we say, with an extra dimension. The later Jane, working more closely, tightening her grip upon the reins, could not have created him. Two comparisons will serve to point the difference. Sir Walter Elliot, for example, is good, a stiff but very effective little sketch (there is certainly not enough of him), and his few snatches of talk have a fine savour, the very accents of bland self-approval ; but he is not limned with any gusto ; his creator does not love him (and I do not mean approve of him, of course) sufficiently to indulge him ; he does what he has to do in furthering the plot of *Persuasion* and that is all ; he exists for the sake of the story. Of Mr. Woodhouse we see a great deal more ; he is indulged here and there and Miss Austen's talk *about* him, her description of his valetudinarianism, is among her best comic passages ; but he himself only falls gently into his place in the Highbury group ; after the first description of him, we know what to expect and receive no more than we expect ; he is a stagnant pond rather than a gushing spring of folly. But Mr. Collins comes to life the moment we meet him, nay, before we meet him, for he is all there in that letter which Mr. Bennet reads out at the breakfast table, that letter which makes Elizabeth remark : " He must be an oddity, I think. I cannot make him out.—There is something very pompous in his style.—And what can he mean by apologising for being next in the entail ?—We cannot suppose he would help it if he could.—Can he be sensible man, sir ? " And Mr. Bennet, that connoisseur of absurdity, answers for all of us when he replies : " No, my dear, I think not. I have great hopes of finding him quite the reverse. There is a mixture of servility and self-importance in his letter, which promises well. I am impatient to see him." We are all impatient to see him. When he arrives upon the scene, he comes to life immediately and remains alive.

Although we feel that we know what he will do and say next, yet he always goes beyond our expectations just as absurd people in real life do ; we know the kind of thing he will say, yet we could not say it for him (as we could with a lesser comic character), for his absurdity is always a little in advance of what we can possibly imagine. Thus he is, as Mr. Saintsbury once remarked somewhere, a creature " of the highest and most Shakespearian comedy." And being a person of such great lineage, he does not exist simply for the sake of the story (though he plays his part in it), does not fall into his place in the group, but exists in his own right and compels his creator to indulge him all over the place, just as Falstaff black-mailed Shakespeare for scene after scene.

It is not until Mr. Collins has spent a whole evening at the Bennets that Miss Austen describes him, so that she allows us to see him for ourselves and allows Mr. Collins to display himself without any hints and nudges on the part of his creator. This description forms the opening paragraph of Chapter Fifteen, and it is worth noticing that Miss Austen, instead of making the account itself humorous, goes to work coldly, almost scientifically, as if she were describing a somewhat unpleasant insect, and says in effect that, having set Mr. Collins in motion, she intends to let the audience find their own fun :

Mr. Collins was not a sensible man, and the deficiency of Nature had been but little assisted by education or society ; the greatest part of his life having been spent under the guidance of an illiterate and miserly father ; and though he belonged to one of the universities, he had merely kept the necessary terms, without forming at it any useful acquaintance. The subjection in which his father had brought him up had given him originally great humility of manner ; but it was now a good deal counteracted by the self-conceit of a weak head, living in retirement, and the consequential feelings of early and unexpected prosperity. A fortunate chance had recommended him to Lady Catherine de Bourgh when the living of Hunsford was vacant ; and the respect which he felt for her high rank, and his veneration for her as his patroness, mingling with a very good opinion of himself, of his authority as a clergyman, and his right as a rector, made him altogether a mixture of pride and obsequiousness, self-importance and humility.

It is obvious that there is some excellent material here for a highly satirical sketch of the tuft-hunting eighteenth-century parson, a familiar figure easily capable of arousing feelings of disgust or contempt not untinged with amusement ; but such an attitude of disgust or contempt is not one that we can maintain towards any major comic character, or it would not be a major comic character. The superficial view of all comic figures in literature is, of course, that they are contemptible, and good critics who have set out to attack and destroy this view have

sometimes gone to the other extreme in over-emphasising
the lovable aspect of certain great comic characters ;
nevertheless these later critics have been much nearer
the truth, for every humorous personage even of the
second rank is something more than a satirical portrait
or sketch and must do something more than arouse our
disgust or even genial contempt.   By hook or crook a
comic character, to be successful, must be able to draw
a draft on our sympathy that we are willing to meet,
although we may not be aware of the fact that we are
meeting it.   If the question had been put to her, Miss
Austen herself, for all her clear-sightedness, would
probably have said that her purpose was purely satirical ;
as the daughter of a parson, she disliked the patronage
system then prevailing and had a contempt for the time-
servers who helped to bolster up that system, so that she
simply set out to caricature the type in Mr. Collins.
Although she certainly enjoyed him, I doubt if she enjoyed him as we enjoy him now ;   he was too close to her,
too much bound up in her mind with serious questions.
All the intelligent characters in *Pride and Prejudice* are
either bored or annoyed by Mr. Collins.   Elizabeth
Bennet, rather surprisingly perhaps, considering her un-
doubted sense of humour, very quickly finds him almost
intolerable, and even when she is no longer in any danger
of being proposed to again (though what a delightful

danger, at least to us at a distance), she avoids his society. It is true that she goes to stay at the Hunsford parsonage, but that is only for the sake of the change and her friend Charlotte, now Mrs. Collins : absence, we are told, " had increased her desire of seeing Charlotte again, and weakened her disgust of Mr. Collins." Her father, as we know, had great hopes of discovering an exquisite fool in Mr. Collins, and was not disappointed ; he had at least one delightful afternoon and evening, when " he listened to him (Mr. Collins) with the keenest enjoyment, maintaining at the same time the most resolute composure of countenance . . ." ; and we can hardly doubt that the following dialogue was one of Mr. Bennet's golden moments, to be treasured in the memory . Mr. Collins is speaking :

" . . . I have more than once observed to Lady Catherine, that her charming daughter seemed born to be a duchess, and that the most elevated rank, instead of giving her consequence, would be adorned by her.— These are the kind of little things which please her lady-ship, and it is a sort of attention which I feel myself peculiarly bound to pay."

" You judge very properly," said Mr. Bennet, " and it is happy for you that you possess the talent of flattering with delicacy. May I ask whether these pleasing atten-tions proceed from the impulse of the moment, or are the result of previous study ? "

" They arise chiefly from what is passing at the time,

and though I sometimes amuse myself with suggesting
and arranging such little elegant compliments as may be
adapted to ordinary occasions, I always wish to give them
as unstudied an air as possible."

Could any gentleman long dedicated to the quest of the
ridiculous have asked for anything better ? And yet by
the following morning, Mr. Bennet is only too anxious
to see the last of his young relative, and we never find
him anxious to hear any more of Lady Catherine de
Bourgh and Rosings. He, like us, could have *read*
about Mr. Collins for ever, but having to meet him in
the flesh and listen to his unexpurgated talk, he quickly
tired, as we should have done. It is one of the triumphs
of art that it can transform the most colossal bores into
enchanting personages.

Jane Austen presents to us a great company of snobs,
and Mr. Collins is, of course, a member of that company.
But he stands apart from the rest, for he is no ordinary
snob. With him, what we call snobbery has become a
passion, and time-serving and toadyism are raised to a
poetical height. A snob has been defined as a person
who meanly admires mean things, but if we are to accept
this definition, then Mr. Collins escapes, for though he
admires mean things (namely, Lady Catherine de Bourgh
and his own paltry preferment), he does not admire them
meanly. He admires them in a fashion in which few

of us are able to admire anything ; he sees them bathed in the light that never was on land or sea. His position at Hunsford, his standing at Rosings, the affability and condescension of Lady Catherine, these are no longer the means to some end, but are an end in themselves ; they have become the core of his existence ; everything else in life is referred to them and judged by them ; and his admiration, his wonder, and his self-satisfaction have combined to form a ruling passion. Had he been an older man, he would not have been such a magnificent oddity, nor should we have liked him so well ; but he is young ("a tall, heavy looking young man of five and twenty") and he is also in orders. Now young men very often have some ruling passion and become single-minded under its stress, and if the object of their passion is proportionately significant, if they are driven, say, by love or overmastering ambition, they compel our respect and sympathy, and indeed provide us with the material for our tragedies. If, however, the ruling passion has somehow gathered about a Lady Catherine and her quadrille table, the effect is particularly ludicrous. But it is heightened again by the fact that Mr. Collins is also a clergyman. Priests of all kinds have always been ripe subjects for comedy simply because there is something distinctly comic, at least to disinterested observers, in the contrast between the high solemnity of their office and their frailties as men. We can never quite reconcile ourselves to the fact that a man may represent the Creator and yet be sadly put out of humour by a badly cooked vegetable. When, therefore, we hear of Mr. Collins for the first time and read, in the letter he sent to Mr. Bennet, such a passage as this :

My mind, however, is now made up on the subject, for having received ordination at Easter, I have been so fortunate as to be distinguished by the patronage of the Right Honourable Lady Catherine de Bourgh, widow of Sir Lewis de Bourgh, whose bounty and beneficence has preferred me to the valuable rectory of this parish, where it shall be my earnest endeavour to demean myself with grateful respect towards her Ladyship, and be ever ready to perform those rites and ceremonies which are instituted by the Church of England. . . .

we are immediately tickled by the evident disproportion. The Lady Catherine-Rosings-Hunsford combination has not only taken a place only to be worthily occupied by, say, Helen of Troy, or the conquest of the East in a young man's dreams ; but as the young man happens to be in orders, it has also become more important than God. Mr. Collins is a Romantic, for all his moments have value because of one secret enchantment ; there trills in his heart " that time-devouring nightingale " (as Stevenson, defending his Lantern Bearers, calls the hidden poetry in men) ; but unfortunately for our gravity, though not, I hope, for our sympathy, we happen to know that the glamorous bird is no other than our old acquaintance Lady Catherine de Bourgh, who is gilding Mr. Collins' hours by inviting him to her quadrille table or giving him advice about " some shelves in the closets upstairs."

This simple and by no means entirely prosaic soul, having taken possession so early of his heart's desire, is so happy, so lost in wonder at his own good fortune, that he is a man apart and the happiest creature in the book, for all his solemn airs. He may bore other people, but nothing bores him. He comes into Hertfordshire, to visit the Bennets, as if he were entering fairyland. He admires the furniture, the pictures, the cooking, and his five fair cousins ; everywhere he goes, he finds something to admire and to wonder at ; he cannot dance at all well, but he is willing to try ; he does not know how to play whist, but sits down to it with pleasure and declares that he will be glad to improve himself ; if one young lady is not eligible, he immediately transfers his affections to the next : nothing comes amiss. How should it when he is still the vicar of Hunsford and still under the kindly patronage of no less a person than Lady Catherine ? Just as a happy lover asks the world to rejoice with him and sees everything by the light of his mistress's eyes, so Mr. Collins, secretly dazed and moon-

struck under his elaborate show of formality, has allowed
the little imagination he has to be entirely dominated by
the wonder of it all ; he is so delighted at being in his
own place that you cannot expect him to be able to put
himself in anybody else's place ; he is really a little boy
pretending to be grown up ; and his apparent snobbery
and time-serving are so gross, open, palpable, so all-
pervading in their influence, that they cease to be snobbery
and time-serving and together become a new kind of
passion, an unheard-of poetry, only compelling laughter
because it feeds upon such strange food and celebrates
so magnificently such paltry triumphs. Though super-
ficially he may be regarded as a particularly mean and
foolish toady, yet his natural stupidity, his youth, his
wonder at the position in which he finds himself, his
single-mindedness, all these contrive to transform him
into an enthusiastic innocent He is not only the
happiest creature in the book, he is also the least sophis-
ticated. Mrs. Bennet, for example, is silly and shallow
enough, and all her designs are sufficiently transparent,
but compared with Mr. Collins she is almost deep. This
is well illustrated by that delicious snatch of dialogue
between the two when Elizabeth, much to her mother's
disgust, has refused Mr. Collins :

This information, however, startled Mrs. Bennet ;
—she would have been glad to be equally satisfied that her

daughter had meant to encourage him by protesting against his proposals, but she dared not believe it, and could not help saying so.

" But, depend upon it, Mr. Collins," she added, " that Lizzy shall be brought to reason. I will speak to her about it myself directly. She is a very headstrong, foolish girl, and does not know her own interest ; but I will *make* her know it."

" Pardon me for interrupting you, madam," cried Mr. Collins ; " but if she is really headstrong and foolish, I know not whether she would altogether be a very desirable wife to a man in my situation, who naturally looks for happiness in the marriage state. If, therefore, she actually persists in rejecting my suit, perhaps it were better not to force her into accepting me, because if liable to such defects of temper, she could not contribute much to my felicity."

" Sir, you quite misunderstand me," said Mrs. Bennet, alarmed. " Lizzy is only headstrong in such matters as these. In everything else she is as good-natured a girl as ever lived. I will go directly to Mr. Bennet, and we shall very soon settle it with her, I am sure."

But this little dialogue inevitably leads us back to what is the best comic proposal in literature.

It is in this declaration to Elizabeth that Mr. Collins is discovered in his glory ; the pompousness and delicious air of absurdity that always run through his speech are here to perfection ; his bland and innocent self-approval, his lack of imagination or understanding of other persons' feelings and points of view, his almost

idiotic reasonableness, these and other traits are nowhere
displayed to better advantage ; nor can his own curious
scale of values, the disproportion between his feelings
and their objects, the whole *topsyturvyness* of him, be
seen so clearly in any other place.   He begins, it will be
remembered, by assuring Elizabeth that what he imagines
to be her modesty (it is actually her distaste for his society)
only adds to her charm.   Nothing could be better calcu-
lated to annoy a frank, high-spirited girl like Elizabeth,
of course, than such a smirking comment upon her
imaginary coyness.   But Mr. Collins only goes from
bad to worse.   With that bland assumption of masculine
superiority, at which Miss Austen is always having sly
digs, he points out that as soon as he entered the house
(he has only been there a few days) he singled her out as
the companion of his future life.   Having got so far,
he checks himself, much to Elizabeth's amusement,
and remarks :

" But before I am run away with by my feelings on
this subject, perhaps it would be advisable for me to state
my reasons for marrying—and, moreover, for coming
into Hertfordshire with the design of selecting a wife,
as I certainly did."

What follows must have been funny enough to Miss
Austen and her friends, but it is probably even funnier
to us now, because we have more romantic views of

marriage   It is obvious that though a man may have
many reasons for marrying, the only one of interest to
the lady he is proposing to is his desire for the enjoyment
of her society and person, particularly, at the present
time, her person.   But Mr. Collins, innocently floundering further and further into the mire, has only one
passion, as we have seen, and has not sufficient interest
and imagination left to become a lover, so he proceeds
to give reasons that leave his hearer very cold indeed :

"My reasons for marrying are, first, that I think it
a right thing for every clergyman in easy circumstances
(like myself) to set the example of matrimony in his parish ;
secondly, that I am convinced it will add very greatly
to my happiness ; and thirdly, which perhaps I ought
to have mentioned earlier, that it is the particular advice
and recommendation of the very noble lady whom I
have the honour of calling patroness.   Twice has she
condescended to give me her opinion (unasked too !) on
this subject ; and it was but the very Saturday night
before I left Hunsford—between our pools at quadrille,
while Mrs. Jenkinson was arranging Miss de Bourgh's
footstool, that she said, ' Mr. Collins, you must marry.
A clergyman like you must marry.—Chuse properly,
chuse a gentlewoman for *my* sake ; and for your *own*,
let her be an active, useful sort of person, not brought up
high, but able to make a small income go a good way.
This is my advice.   Find such a woman as soon as you
can, bring her to Hunsford, and I will visit her.' "

He then goes on to point out, very characteristically,

that the promise of Lady Catherine's notice is not the least of the advantages he can offer his wife. All this shows his innocence and want of sophistication, his sheer inability to leave off wondering at his own blessed condition and to look at things from another person's point of view ; but his further blundering shows it even better, for he goes steadily from bad to worse. His remark that, being the heir to Mr. Bennet's estate, he felt it almost his duty to choose one of his cousins, is extraordinarily tactless, for no girl wishes to be pitied or condescended to, and Elizabeth can hardly have relished the bland reference to the possibility of her father's early death. But still more tactless, a stupidity beyond any ordinary snob and time-server, is his further statement that he is indifferent to money and knows very well that Elizabeth's portion will be little or nothing. It is at this point that the infuriated girl interrupts him and hastily declines his offer. Mr. Collins, however, so single-minded that it is impossible for him to believe that any rational creature would willingly decline the delights of Hunsford and Rosings, puts on a delicious air of sophistication, like a small boy imitating his elders, and hints that the refusal is mere coyness. He declares that he is not discouraged This, of course, only increases Elizabeth's annoyance, and she not only declines again but plays a trump card by declaring that Lady

Catherine would find her "in every respect ill qualified for the situation."

This is a terrible suggestion, and it pulls Mr. Collins up short :

"Were it certain that Lady Catherine would think so," said Mr. Collins very gravely—"but I cannot imagine that her ladyship would at all disapprove of you. . . ."

He will speak for her. Miss Bennet then declines his offer again in no measured terms, but the importunate gentleman will not believe that he is refused. It is not that he is conceited and thinks so well of himself that he cannot understand a girl's rejecting him ; it is not himself, his appearance, manners, and so forth, that he is in love with, but his situation in life, the patronage of Lady Catherine and his position at Hunsford ; so that his inability to understand Elizabeth's refusal is not the result of mere blind conceit but of a kind of almost selfless devotion, a devotion, as we have seen, that is only comic because its objects are so preposterous. When, Elizabeth finally exasperated, declares that she does not know how to convince him that she has refused him, he replies, magnificently :

"You must give me leave to flatter myself, my dear cousin, that your refusal of my addresses is merely words of course. My reasons for believing it are briefly these :—It does not appear to me that my hand is unworthy your acceptance, or that the establishment I can offer would be other than highly desirable.   My situation in life, my connections with the family of De Bourgh, and my relationship to your own, are circumstances highly in my favour ; and you should take it into further consideration, that in spite of your manifold attractions, it is by no means certain that another offer of marriage may ever be made you.   Your portion is unhappily so small that it will in all likelihood undo the effects of your loveliness and amiable qualifications. . . ."

This speech is a model of what not to say to a lady, a monument of tactlessness, and no ingenious time-server, but only a simpleton, could have made it.   If there is a certain resentment dawning in it, and there is no doubt that for a time Mr. Collins was very resentful towards Elizabeth, it is, I think, not so much the result of ordinary wounded vanity as of a more general passion springing to the defence of its object.   It is not so much himself, William Collins, who has been rejected, as Lady Catherine and Rosings and Hunsford, the beloved idea in which they are grouped, and it is this, if anything, that makes the young and solemn enthusiast resentful.   He is already, in his own queer way, a lover, not of a young lady but of an idea that includes, among other things, a foolish old lady ; and he is bewildered and somewhat resentful because another person has refused to share his enthusiasm.   He cannot, will not, believe it ; it is incredible, monstrous.

In the later chapters, when we journey to Hunsford with Elizabeth, we discover Mr. Collins, now comfortably married, in the character of the happy enthusiast   Elizabeth, we are told, " was prepared to see him in his glory," and she is not disappointed ; Mr. Collins is in his glory and remains there.   He takes his guest into the garden and points out every view :

He could number the fields in every direction, and could tell how many trees there were in the most distant clump.   But of all the views which his garden, or which the country or the kingdom could boast, none were to be compared with the prospect of Rosings, afforded by an opening in the trees that bordered the park nearly opposite the front of his house.

This is to have an overwhelming enthusiasm, to be something, at least, of a poet, and when we see how Mr. Collins is perpetually engaged at a feast of happiness, how he can be thrown into a kind of ecstasy by the smallest events, we must begin to wonder whether it is not better to have such an enthusiasm as he had, ridiculous as it may be, than to have none at all.   How eagerly he assures his visitors that they will soon have the honour of seeing Lady Catherine at church on Sunday and possibly at Rosings.   How delighted he is when an invitation arrives from that gracious lady for the whole party :

" I confess," said he, " that I should not have been at

all surprised by her ladyship's asking us on Sunday to drink tea and spend the evening at Rosings. I rather expected from my knowledge of her affability, that it would happen. But who could have foreseen such an attention as this ? Who could have imagined that we should receive an invitation to dine there (an invitation, moreover, including the whole party) so immediately after your arrival ! "

He can talk of nothing else and tells them all what to expect so that they will not be overpowered by the sight of such magnificence. When the evening arrives, he is in a happy fever of expectation, hurries them all into their clothes, walks through the park on air, and spends delicious hours pointing out the beauty of this and the splendour of that. There is no need to follow him ; all that remains to be said is that all the other characters in the book together cannot produce such a spectacle of solid happiness as this is ; and it continues throughout the visit, until the final speech, when he tells Elizabeth how delighted he has been to have introduced her into superior society, how she can bear witness in Hertfordshire to Lady Catherine's great attentions to Mrs. Collins, how he hopes she will be as happy in her marriage as he is (he has not forgotten his proposal and its reception), for he and his dear Charlotte have but one mind and one way of thinking. This last is hardly the truth, but it is much nearer the truth than Miss Bennet imagines, for it is quite clear that Charlotte, who had, we imagine, few illusions about Mr. Collins when she married him and regarded the Lady Catherine and Rosings' enthusiasm much as Elizabeth herself regarded it, has come at last to think more or less as her husband does ; once more enthusiasm has conquered common-sense, and Mr. Collins has played Don Quixote to his wife's Sancho. Jane Austen was no friend to romance, and she would certainly be surprised if one of her avowedly satirical figures were pressed into service in a defence of the romantic attitude ; yet the fact remains that this ridiculous Mr. Collins of hers, with his snobberies soaring sky-high, lost in wonder, innocently and ostentatiously marching under the banner of toadyism until it is no longer the banner of toadyism, this Mr. Collins is at once a child of romance and perhaps the happiest creature in all her pages. We would rather be in ecstasy with him at Rosings than bored with Darcy in the theatre and the ball-room, for though no sensible person would share Mr. Collins' enthusiasms, and admire what he admires, every one must envy his state of mind, which follows that of the poet and gives significance to things that never were significant before and sees nothing, in the light of its enthusiasm, that is too dull to be noticed ; and so can cry out for joy at the sight of a phaeton passing the gate and know strange ecstasies at a dowager's tea-table.

PRINCE SEITHENYN

THAT curious blend of romance and satire, *The Misfortunes of Elphin*, contains the quintessential Peacock, the very marrow of his humour. Its unique flavour comes from the delicious incongruity of subject and treatment, for the sources of the tale, the two old stories that Peacock has fused into one continuous narrative, are from the early Welsh legends and are very vague, very Celtic, very legendary, whereas nothing could be less Celtic, less in the spirit of legend than the story that Peacock tells with such smooth irony. The genuine romantic feeling is not entirely lost (Peacock never did lose it), but the narrative is perhaps best described as a romantic outline filled in with satire, as if a kindlier Swift or a more robust Anatole France had worked upon the synopsis of one of the Waverley Novels. The two legends that Peacock used are that of Elphin and the inundation of Gwaelod, which is mentioned in a note by Lady Guest, and that of Taliesin, the great bard, whose history is given at length in the *Mabinogion*. Actually, the figure of Seithenyn only appears in the first legend, the inundation of Gwaelod, but Peacock, having found him and made much of him, fortunately could not let him go and contrived that Seithenyn should play a part in the story of Taliesin.   Peacock's Seithenyn, however, owes very little to the vague figure of the legend.   It is true that the legendary character, shadowy though he may be, is a person of some consequence. The *Triads* refer to him as one of " the three immortal drunkards of the Isle of Britain," no mean reference when we remember that at no time in the history of this island has such a reputation been easily earned, for it argues both unusual application and uncommon powers. We know too that it was Seithenyn and his drunkenness that were responsible for the present configuration of the coast of Wales, for it was he, and no other, who was in charge of the embankment that protected the low-lying plain of Gwaelod from the sea, and, as a result of his negligence, this embankment was broken down by the spring tides, which overwhelmed the plain of Gwaelod so thoroughly that its pleasant pastures have remained ever since at the bottom of Cardigan Bay.   But while there is here a suggestion for an unusually picturesque scene, a suggestion that Peacock turned to good account in the third chapter of *The Misfortunes of Elphin*, there is hardly more than the flimsiest sketch, the merest hint, of a comic character, so that Seithenyn must be considered

Peacock's own creation, and is, in fact, his masterpiece
—an immortal drunkard indeed.

Fanatical temperance reformers are not usually great
readers, but even they, I imagine, would be loth to drive
strong drink out of literature, in which a love of good
liquor has played a notable part. Drunkenness in good
literature is not like drunkenness in real life ; it is subtly
spiritualised ; the sparkle, bloom, and fragrance of wine,
the jolly comradeship of the bottle, the Bacchic ardours
and ecstasies, are all there, without the hiccoughs and
the carbuncles, the sagging mouth and the shaking hand
We feel that the great comic drunkards of literature are
something more than mere bibbers and topers, creatures
of the tap-room, who chance to make amusing remarks
when they are in their cups. They are comic poets
and lovers, and the wine they drink is no earthly liquor
but is of starry vintage, looted from the cellar of the
gods, having divine properties like Falstaff's sherris-sack,
which " ascends me into the brain ; drives me there all
the foolish and dull and crudy vapours which environ
it ; makes it apprehensive, quick, forgetive, full of
nimble, fiery and delectable shapes ; which, delivered
o'er to the voice, the tongue, which is the birth, becomes
excellent wit." This passage explains why literature
refuses to exile her mighty drinkers. They go to the
bottle not for oblivion, not to be soused until they are as

dull and forgetful as the beasts of the field, not so that they may be less than men, but so that they may be more than men, divine for an hour or so, seated above the ruins of Death and Time and Change like the gods themselves, bandying immortal jests. We can no more find it in our hearts to condemn them for letting their affairs rot while they go in pursuit of good liquor and good company than we can to despise Romeo because he too is neglecting his appointments and offices and has taken to haunting the garden of old Capulet. If Juliet is Romeo's excuse, so too sherris-sack is Falstaff's ; and if it is not possible for many men to discover so much witchery in a chit of a girl as Romeo found in Juliet, so too it is not possible for them to find their liquor so divinely potent as Falstaff found his sherris-sack. Romeo and his kind are lovers of genius ; Falstaff and his kind are drinkers of genius ; the first are drawn near to the gates of Paradise by the pressure of a small white hand or by an exquisite glance, whereas the others, the drinkers, sail away to the Happy Isles on roaring but friendly seas of liquor ; one set is dignified and tragic, the other is undignified and comic, but both, in their devotion, their ecstasies, their wit and poetry, tower above common humanity, in or out of love, drunk or dry. In this company of glorious topers, whose hours of ease are as far above those of ordinary men as are Antony's nights of passion or Hamlet's intense moments of wonder and disgust, who transform the world into one great tavern and reckon fame and fortune a trifling price to pay for the entry there, whose captain is surely the fat knight, is to be found Peacock's Prince Seithenyn, and even in this company he cuts no mean figure.

We never meet him out of his cups : he is always reeling ripe. Undismayed by any change of fortune so long as there is liquor to be had, he staggers through the book flourishing his golden goblet and for ever exclaiming, "*Gwin o eur*—Wine from gold." And he is always at that stage of intoxication which might be called the argumentative and dialectical, when the drinker, floundering in a happy alcoholic mist, attempts that almost insane clarity of speech and that strictly syllogistic method of reasoning which seem to be peculiar to inebriates, philosophers, and certain angry women. Such persons rise above common-sense, which they despise, and end by talking a peculiar kind of nonsense of their own because they are anxious, at all costs, to proffer the pure unadulterated essence of reason. They worship the ideal form, let the spirit wander where it will. An intelligent, sober man is usually content to reason rather loosely so long as his premises are sound and his conclusions sensible ; he keeps a pragmatic eye upon his argument and does not trouble himself overmuch about the form in which it is set forth, being only anxious to arrive somewhere and not to commit himself to absurdities. But drink and the philosophies of the absolute, flying to the head, crumble away common-sense, dim the pragmatic eye, and give the devotee a shining vision of pure dialectic, in contrast with which mere reality is a sordid muddle that can be left out of reckoning ; the stage is now set for the comic old drama of *All for Reason ; or the World well lost for a syllogism.* And this is the stage of intoxication at which we always find Seithenyn. He has too, like so many of Peacock's characters, a certain crisp rhythm, a tang, in his speech, and this adds just the necessary sparkle of salt to his utterance and gives it the perfect flavour of absurdity. Every considerable speech he makes carries with it the most imposing air of reason, and yet every one ends by being nonsense, matter so tangled that it is impossible to unravel it. Among the great bibulous fools, he takes first place as a dialectician and probably he was long since appointed their official apologist. As a specimen of his characteristic topsyturvy method of reasoning, there is nothing better than his denial of his own death in the scene in which Taliesin discovers him, the supposedly drowned Prince, acting as a butler to King Melvas :

After a silence, which he designed to be very dignified and solemn, the stranger spoke again : " I am the man."

"What man ? " said Taliesin.

"The man," replied his entertainer, "of whom you have spoken so disparagingly ; Seithenyn ap Seithyn Saidi."

"Seithenyn," said Taliesin, "has slept twenty years under the waters of the western sea, as King Gwythno's Lamentations have made known to all Britain."

"They have not made it known to me," said Seithenyn, "for the best of all reasons, that one can only know the truth ; for, if that which we think we know is not truth, it is something which we do not know. A man cannot know his own death ; for, while he knows anything he is alive ; at least, I never heard of a dead man who knew anything, or pretended to know anything : if he had so pretended, I should have told him to his face he was no dead man."

But Seithenyn's great scene is in the earlier chapters, when we meet him in his own castle. He holds the office of Lord High Commissioner of Royal Embankment, and, we are told, "he executed it as a personage so denominated might be expected to do : he drank the profits, and he left the embankment to his deputies, who left it to their assistants, who left it to itself." Along the great sea-wall there are watch-towers, with companies of guards under the command of various officers, who are in their turn subordinate to Seithenyn in his central castle. The officer in charge of a watch-tower at one of the extreme ends of the embankment is a certain Teithrin ap Tathral, who, being new to public service or somewhat simple-minded, goes to the trouble of keeping his own portion of the embankment in excellent condition. Chancing to discover, however, that the rest of the embankment is by no means in the same condition as his own charge, he is considerably dismayed, and hastens inland to warn the King. Accompanied by the King's son, Elphin, a very public-spirited young man, Teithrin returns to pay a visit of remonstrance to the Lord High Commissioner. They arrive at Seithenyn's castle at night. Outside, the sea, grey, restless, is crumbling away the ruinous mound of the embankment ; but inside, the torches blaze, the sound of harp and song bursts through the doors, and wine and wassail go round. A jovial chorus is singing " The Circling of the Mead Horns " :

> Seithenyn ap Seithyn, the generous, the bold,
> Drinks the wine of the stranger from vessels of gold ;
> But we from the horn, the blue silver-rimmed horn,
> Drink the ale and the mead in our fields that were born. . . .

and high above his followers, high, indeed, above reality and the pressure of circumstance, sits the great Seithenyn, flourishing his golden goblet.

" You are welcome all four," he cries, when he notices the two strangers. Then when he learns that one of his visitors is the son of his master, he endeavours " to straighten himself into perpendicularity, and to stand steadily on his legs." But being very drunk indeed, he finds this too difficult and ends by dropping into his chair like a plummet, at the same time, with the large and generous gestures of the inebriated, waving his royal guest into the seat at his right hand, and, after some effort, managing to compose himself into a dignified attitude that leaves " his right hand at liberty, for the ornament of his eloquence and the conduct of his liquor." Meanwhile, his other visitor, Teithrin, remains at the end of the hall, only to be remonstrated with by Seithenyn, who exclaims with drunken gravity and characteristic confusion : " Come on, man, come on. What if you be not the son of a king, you are the guest of Seithenyn ap Seithyn Saidi. The most honourable place to the most honourable guest, and the next most honourable place to the next most honourable guest ; the least honourable guest above the most honourable inmate ; and, where there are but two guests, be the most honourable who he may, the least honourable of the two is next in honour to the most honourable of the two, because there are no more but two ; and where there are two, there can be nothing between. Therefore sit, and drink. *Gwin o eur* : wine from gold." Food is then placed before the two visitors, but Seithenyn begs to be excused from joining them in their repast as he is troubled with a feverishness and parching of the mouth, a complaint that necessitates frequent moistening of the lips and impedes his saying, " All I would say, and will say before I have done, in token of my loyalty and fealty to your highness and your highness's house."

Meanwhile His Highness, who is a crude young man and does not realise that his host and all the company are floating away on seas of liquor to ideal realms and do not wish to be reminded of the reality that ought to have faded away over the horizon long ago, drinks nothing but comes, with something like brutality, to the business in hand. " Prince Seithenyn," he remarks, " I have visited you on a subject of deep moment. Reports have been brought to me, that the embankment, which has been so long entrusted to your care, is in a state of dangerous decay."

Secure in the wisdom that years and the bottle and a conservative mind give a man, Seithenyn sees that his visitor is pathetically young and painfully sober and that, having swallowed little so far in life but facts, has yet to realise that things in this world are strangely complex and only to be fully understood by a mind that has been mellowed and made subtle by the grape. Seithenyn, then, deals gently with him, and answers him as so many fine old conservative apologists have answered young would-be reformers. " Decay," he observes, " is one thing, and danger is another. Everything that is old must decay. That the embankment is old, I am free to confess ; that it is somewhat rotten in parts, I will not altogether deny ; that it is any the worse for that, I do most sturdily gainsay. It does its business well : it works well : it keeps out the water from the land, and it lets in the wine upon the High Commission of Embankment. Cup-bearer, fill. Our ancestors were wiser than we : they built it in their wisdom ; and if we should be so rash as to try to mend it, we should only mar it."

Then Teithrin, that matter-of-fact person, takes a hand, remarking : " The stonework is sapped and mined : the piles are rotten, broken, and dislocated : the floodgates and sluices are leaky and creaky." Seithenyn remains undismayed by such crude tactics ; he grasps the nettle : " That is the beauty of it. Some parts of it are rotten, and some parts of it are sound." But this is quite beyond Prince Elphin, who takes refuge in his rank and observes, regally : " It is well that some parts are sound : it were better that all were so."

" So I have heard some people say before," Seithenyn, now thoroughly roused, replies ; " perverse people, blind to venerable antiquity : that very unamiable sort of people, who are in the habit of indulging their reason." (This last phrase is rather a poor stroke of Peacock's and is not in character.)   " But I say, the parts that are rotten give elasticity to those that are sound : they give them elasticity, elasticity, elasticity. If it were all sound it would break by its own obstinate stiffness : the soundness is checked by the rottenness, and the stiffness is balanced by the elasticity. There is nothing so dangerous as innovation. See the waves in the equinoctial storms, dashing and clashing, roaring and pouring, spattering and battering, rattling and battling against it. I would not be so presumptuous as to say, I could build anything that would stand against them half an hour ; and here this immortal old work, which God forbid the finger of modern mason should bring into jeopardy, this immortal work has stood for centuries, and will stand for centuries more, if we let it alone. It is well : it works well : let well alone. Cup-bearer, fill. It was half-rotten when I was born, and that is a conclusive reason why it should be three parts rotten when I die."

At this point, we are told, the whole body of the High Commission, now very drunk, roared approbation, as well they might. Seithenyn resumed : " And after all, the worst that could happen would be the overflow of a springtide, for that was the worst that happened before the embankment was thought of ; and, if the high water should come in, as it did before, the low water would go out again, as it did before. We should be no deeper in it than our ancestors were, and we could mend as easily as they could make."

He is interrupted by Teithrin, who observes that " the level of the sea is materially altered." But Seithenyn will have none of it. "The level of the sea!" he exclaims. "Who ever heard of such a thing as altering the level of the sea? Alter the level of that bowl of wine before you, in which, as I sit here, I see a very ugly reflection of your very good-looking face. Alter the level of that : drink up the reflection : let me see the face without the reflection, and leave the sea to level itself."

"Not to level the embankment," Teithrin replies.

"Good, very good," remarks Seithenyn, who is by this time washed up on the shores of the Happy Isles. "I love a smart saying, though it hits at me. But whether yours is a smart saying or no, I do not very clearly see ; and, whether it hits at me or no, I do not very sensibly feel. But all is one. Cup-bearer, fill." Then, looking as intently as it is possible for a man in his condition to do at Teithrin, he goes on : "I think I have seen something very like you before. There was a fellow here the other day very like you : he stayed here some time : he would not talk : he did nothing but drink : he used to drink till he could not stand, and then he went walking about the embankment. I suppose he thought it wanted mending ; but he did not say anything. If he had, I should have told him to embank his own throat, to keep the liquor out of that. That would have posed him : he could not have answered that : he would not have had a word to say for himself after that."

"He must have been a miraculous person," observes Teithrin, who is clearly the libelled visitor, "to walk when he could not stand." But Seithenyn is too far gone for such quibbles to have any effect. He remarks : "All is one for that. Cup-bearer, fill ! "

This will not do for Elphin, who sees that the old toper must be sternly rebuked and so speaks out plainly : "Prince Seithenyn, if I was not aware that wine speaks in the silence of reason, I should be astonished at your strange vindication of your neglect of duty, which I take shame to myself for not having sooner known and remedied. The wise bard has well observed, 'Nothing is done without the eye of the king.' "

Poised perilously but deliciously upon the very edge of oblivion, the deeply soused Seithenyn makes one last effort and plunges into his final speech of the evening : "I am very sorry that you see things in a wrong light : but we will not quarrel, for three reasons : first, because you are the son of the king, and may do and say what you please without any one having a right to be displeased : second, because I never quarrel with a guest, even if he grows riotous in his cups : third, because there is nothing to quarrel about ; and perhaps that is the best reason of the three ; or, rather, the first is the best, because you are the son of the king ; and the third is the second, that is, the second best, because there is nothing to quarrel about : and the second is nothing to the purpose, because, though guests will grow riotous in their cups, in spite of my good orderly example, God forbid I should say that is the case with you. And I completely agree in the truth of your remark, that reason speaks in the silence of wine." At this point, making a too vehement gesture, Seithenyn drops his goblet, and in endeavouring to pick it up loses his balance and all his dignity and falls prostrate on the floor. The whole body of the High Commission rise to uplift their fallen chief, but as they are as drunk as he is, they too fall prostrate over the benches and upturned tables and all is confusion   Seithenyn is carried away by the cup-bearers.

The storm that follows, in which the embankment is washed away and the whole plain overrun by the spring tides, must be sought for in Peacock's own picturesque prose. It is sufficient here to say that Seithenyn is last seen, by Elphin and the others who contrive to escape, plunging into the waves, sword in hand. He disappears into the wild night and, it would seem, out of the fable. But, as we have already seen, he is discovered after the passage of many years acting as butler to King Melvas ; in short, like so many comic characters, just when we have given up hope of meeting him again, up he pops. This popping up in unexpected places is one of the most delightful characteristics of the comic figures, whose world is filled with strange happy encounters. In the world of the tragic figures, that world overburdened by spirit and clouded with doom, no such chance meetings are possible ; we never lose sight of our protagonists, for their feet are clogged by Fate and their every movement is sickeningly inevitable ; the gods twiddle their fingers, the wires slacken or tauten, pull this way or that, and we see the lovely puppets move through their several agonies until the curtain falls and the darkness covers them. But in the comic world, whose very essence is rollicking freedom, for cause and effect have been huddled away and Destiny stands giggling helplessly in a corner, life is brimmed with chance meetings and old friends are for ever coming out of the blue. A remembered voice floats through the tavern window, a quaint shadow falls across the garden walk, the lamp-light suddenly illumines a monstrous nose, a gaping mouth, and hey presto !—here is our odd acquaintance once more, him that we last saw, years and leagues away, ruffling it in the Boar's Head, Eastcheap, or climbing down from the Rochester coach to drink a hot brandy-and-water, or leaping from the walls of his crumbling castle, sword in hand, into the cauldron of the spring tide.

Not only does Seithenyn pop up unexpectedly in the hall of King Melvas, but after we imagine that we have lost him again, up he pops once more. Taliesin, in his wanderings, has occasion to visit the Abbey of Avallon, and when he inquires for the Abbot, he is told that that dignitary is "confessing a penitent." Gaining admission, he finds the Abbot sitting at a small table on which stand an enormous vase and a golden goblet, a goblet that we have seen before and recognise as the property of our old friend Seithenyn, who is, of course, the penitent in question. From this time forward, Seithenyn wanders in and out of the action, goblet in hand. It is true that he refrains from displaying to the full his skill in dialectics in the discussions at which he is present ; but he is usually able to persuade the various disputants that they are "a cup too low." "Take a little more," he cries to the Abbot, who admits that he takes a little wine medicinally. "That is the true quantity. Wine is my medicine ; and my quantity is a little more. A little more." Does a member of the company see difficulties before him, then Seithenyn is on hand to advise : " Screw yourself with another goblet, you will find the difficulty smooth itself off wonderfully. Wine from gold has a sort of double light, that illuminates a dark path miraculously." If it is admitted that a certain favourable proposition "is nearly true," then Seithenyn fills up again and remarks, "A little more and it will become quite true," and sees, with something of the satisfaction of the creative artist, the proposition gradually ripening into absolute truth. In the end, when all things are settled, he obtains the post of second butler to King Arthur himself and performs his duties, which have to do with the sampling, purchase or commandeering, and transportation of liquor, with unusual zeal.

Leaving Seithenyn happily swaying behind the Table Round, we have leisure to remark more than one level of humour in the scene described at length, the scene in Seithenyn's castle. When *The Misfortunes of Elphin* was being written (it was first published in 1829), Peacock was associated, though not intimately, with the Mills and their friends, the Philosophical Radicals, and was at the time something of a Radical himself, as all readers of his earlier tales must have remarked. It is not surprising, then, that this scene was accepted as a Radical satire upon the contemporary Tory attitude, and that Seithenyn's defence of his policy of doing nothing was taken as a parody of Canning's speeches against Parliamentary reform, the embankment, of course, playing the part of the British Constitution. This is the first level, that of topical political satire. The second level is still one of satire, but we have now dug below the immediate political appeal and can discover in the scene the opposition of two familiar types of mind. Seithenyn becomes a caricature of those conservative-minded persons who will not have anything changed partly because they have a real veneration for the past and partly because they are both fearful and indolent : it is worth remarking that the passage of years transformed Peacock himself into such a person. But we have nothing to do with either of these levels because humour and not satire is our concern. There is a third level underlying these, and it is that of genuine humour, the Comic Absolute, not touching off a given situation nor ridiculing a certain mode of thought, but working—or rather, exploding—through character. Seithenyn dominates the scene, and it is he who has us in thrall. We see him trying to make his reason serve his idleness, his intellect minister to his thirst, and we ought to despise him. Certainly if he were merely a creature too sodden in drink to use his wits, we should despise him ; but we feel that he is above reason rather than below it ; he has escaped from our world into some other, some Cloud-Cuckoodom of liquor and good company that we have never entered but have glimpsed in those moments when we have let our obligations look after themselves and have taken a moral holiday. And there he remains, or, at least, there his spirit remains, for he himself may be still serving as second butler to King Arthur in his invisible Avallon and perhaps to this day all the wine of the Round Table passes through his hands—or down his throat. It may be that if we haunted the Welsh Marches long enough we might yet hear him cry *Gwin o eur*, and catch the flash of his goblet as the old ghosts of chivalry gather about their table or depart, after a stirrup-cup, on their spectral quests.

THE TWO WELLERS

THERE is one queer little period in our literature that has never been adequately discussed by the critics. Roughly we may say that it began in the 'twenties of the last century and ended somewhere in the 'forties ; and it may be described, shortly, as the period of high spirits, or, if you will, the period of plentiful spirits and high jinks. The world, with the universe still in attendance upon it, was safe for a moment ; there was still leisure, time to do everything ; the old picturesque world had not yet crumbled, and the railways, hurling top-hatted gentlemen from Birmingham to London at no less a speed than twenty miles an hour, had not yet driven the coaches from the road nor the landlords of coaching inns, straddling before immense quantities of cheap liquor, out of business ; and ideas, beyond a gentlemanly interest in animal magnetism or phrenology, were infrequent and unfashionable, and Darwin had not yet told his grim tale of the species, nor had Mr. Arnold produced, somewhat disdainfully, his culture. England was more an island than it had been for centuries, almost a separate continent that was not on speaking terms with Europe, and happy in its seas of rum punch and old brown East India sherry, it drained its glasses, ate its pudding and Stilton, bred its eccentrics and cracked its jokes in a provincial and almost bucolic ecstasy. This period produced a literature of its own that is to be distinguished from what came before and what followed after by its high spirits ; these were the days of Barham, Hood, Lever, Surtees, Theodore Hook, Marryat, Peacock, Warren, Walker and his *Original*, and a hundred more ; even criticism was troubled by the prevailing spirit, and so we had Christopher North and his roistering *Noctes*. The innumerable volumes that these gentlemen produced, between bottle and bottle as it were, shadowed forth a world that was really a reflection of the paradise of, say, a typical lieutenant of dragoons, a world of galloping horses, hot brandy-and-water, oysters, practical jokes, devilled kidneys (against which Poe protested so passionately in his attack upon Lever), funny stories, inn parlours, quaint bewhiskered rascals, bobbing chambermaids, negus and macaroons, idiotic foreigners (usually counts and barons), comic red-nosed and predatory spinsters, gouty old gentlemen, and very perfunctory love affairs. At its worst, nothing could be more stupid than this literature, which compels the reader to dance attendance upon half-witted militia

men and horse dealers and dandies in their dreary half-
witted revels, knowing that not a single idea or a really
amusing character or even an entertaining remark will
ever show a sail above the sickening flood of brandy-and-
water.   At its best, in spite of innumerable faults of
taste and a lack of ideas, this literature of masculine high
spirits and comradeship was fleetingly touched with a
kind of poetry, for there was about it a certain boyish
eagerness, a laughing spontaneity, that raised the world
it created above time and change and made it into a
Valhalla of whiskered light dragoons, so that there are
moments when the reader feels that its lounging bloods,
its devil-may-care majors and roguish servants, with their
freedom from ordinary care, their immense appetites
and immeasurable high spirits, their unflagging gusto,
are really gods in disguise.   But it had to be subtly
humanised and mellowed in the mind of genius, like wine
in the brandy cask, before it became great literature ;
and it is fortunate for the period, whose prevalent mood
might otherwise have never had an audience in posterity,
that there came along in the middle of it a certain promising
young reporter who was given a piece of hack work,
common publishers' book-making, to do.   The result,
of course, was *Pickwick Papers*.

So much preamble has been necessary because *Pickwick*,
undoubtedly one of the capital books of our literature and

perhaps one of our contributions to the literature of the world, should be seen against the background of its period to be understood critically ; it is simply our 1830 tale of high spirits raised and illuminated by genius just as *Hamlet* is simply the Elizabethan melodrama raised and illuminated by genius. The real secret of its appeal lies not in the story it tells, the droll situations it presents, not even in the host of comic characters it contains (important as these are), but, as we may guess from the preceding paragraph, in its atmosphere. It is not so much a prose narrative (as, for example, *David Copperfield* is a prose narrative) as a kind of poem, an epic of high spirits and comradeship, feasting and fun. It bathes the world in a light of its own, a rich firelight of humour and good-fellowship, that brings it near to, and gives it the appearance of, one of those ideal worlds with which the imaginations of men, the unhappy brute in them looking for consolation and the god in them reaching towards creation, have for ever played. Mr. Chesterton, who must inevitably be plundered when Dickens is the subject, has made the same point : " But before he (Dickens) wrote a single real story, he had a kind of vision. It was a vision of the Dickens world—a maze of white roads, a map full of fantastic towns, thundering coaches, clamorous market-places, uproarious inns, strange and swaggering figures. That vision was

Pickwick." If, then, the secret of *Pickwick* lies in its comic atmosphere rather than its characters (there are nearly a hundred of them, mostly comic), it will be seen that from our point of view the story is less important than it would first appear. To take one of these fantastic creatures out of the atmosphere in which it is bathed is like plucking out of the green water, which it irradiated with flashes of gold and silver, some little fish that can only gasp and wriggle, colourless and suddenly bereft of its beauty, in the palm of one's hand. The moment they are taken out of the Pickwick world the majority of its comic personages wither and droop ; we are puzzled at our past amusement at such little mechanical toys, these Potts and Leo Hunters and the rest, and yet the moment we put them back they spring into an eccentric life of their own again.

The question, too, is complicated by the fact that Dickens changed his mind about some of the chief personages (really making a subtle change in the character of the book as he found his own feet in its progress), so that they begin as one thing and end as another, and we can only observe them, as it were, on the wing. Thus, Mr. Pickwick is at first a half-witted, pompous old ass, merely an excuse for all manner of practical jokes and horseplay, but by the time we have seen him safely housed at Dulwich he has become a dignified, serious, and very lovable old gentleman, a new kind of hero. A similar change is to be observed in the characters of Messrs. Winkle and Snodgrass, who gradually become heroic and dignified, serious young lovers instead of mere knock-about men. But neither in their first state nor their last are any of these personages really very comic. Among the crowd of minor figures—and there never was such a fantastic crowd assembled together between the covers of one book—one may single out a character here and there in accordance with one's personal taste. Thus, I must own that I have had from earliest youth a tender-ness (not shared by most of my friends) for our old ac-quaintance Jingle, not the forlorn and repentant figure of the later chapters, but the glorious impostor whose extraordinary stacatto conversation kettle-drums us through so many of the early chapters. There is some-thing magnificent about the manner in which this fourth-rate player contrives to take charge of every situation, popping up unexpectedly in so many strange places. His reappearance in the marquee of the All-Muggleton Cricket Team (" This way—this way—capital fun—lots of beer—hogsheads ; rounds of beef—bullocks ; mustard—cartloads ; glorious day—down with you—glad to see you—very ") is one of the great moments of the story, and nothing could be better than the way in which, arriving uninvited from nowhere, he soon contrives to be the most important personage on the field, "eating, drinking, and talking, without cessation." His subsequent reappearances, I must confess, become less and less entertaining ; but I can remember how sorry I used to be that Dickens had not written a whole book describing the adventures of this amusing rascal, and how his repentance at the end used to annoy me : it is as if a magpie should repent.

Excellent, too, are all the medical students. There could hardly be better comic writing than the description of Bob Sawyer's evening party, when Mrs. Raddle, gathering wrath below stairs, plays malignant destiny, and the magnificent Jack Hopkins relates his astonishing anecdotes of hospital life, and the prim man in the cloth boots forgets his story, and Messrs. Gunter and Noddy, yelling "Sir !" at one another, engage in a very ridiculous quarrel, and Mr. Ben Allen, accompanying the Pick-wickians as far as London Bridge at the lamentable conclusion of the party, announces his intention of cutting the throat of any rival of Bob Sawyer's, bursts into tears, crams his hat over his eyes, and returns to knock double knocks at the door of the Borough Market office and take short naps on the steps alternately until daybreak, under the impression that he lives there. And among the crowd of minor characters that come like water and go like wind there is at least one other for whom I have almost a tenderness, and that is the " red-haired, important-looking, sharp-nosed, mysterious-spoken personage, with a bird-like habit of giving his head a jerk every time he said anything," the companion of Mr. Pickwick on his journey to Ipswich, no other than Mr. Peter Magnus. There is something really attractive about the way in which Mr. Magnus finds everything arresting and exciting, as if he had just been born. The fact that he and Mr. Pickwick are both travelling on the outside of the coach to the same town to stay at the very same hotel fills him with ecstasy at such a sequence of co-incidences. Every platitudinous remark he makes (and he expressly states, " I am not fond of anything original ; I don't like it ; don't see the necessity for it ") is brought out with the utmost vehemence and gusto. All the delights, such as the company of fellow-travellers, and all the dangers, such as the possibility of losing luggage, are magnified in his mind. His very name enchants him, and he crows with delight that his initials will serve for Post Meridian and that he is able to sign " hasty notes to intimate acquaintances " simply " Afternoon," which entertains them vastly. It is inconceivable that such a person, wonder itself in red hair and spectacles, can ever have had a single dull moment. Spreading boredom like a blight over the countryside, he himself has never known the horrid state of mind, having chosen for ever to bore and never to be bored.   There may, however, be another explanation.   Mr. Magnus is travelling to Ipswich to propose to a lady, that very lady, middle-aged and yellow curl-papered, into whose bedroom Mr. Pickwick wanders, and so it is possible that what we are seeing is simply Mr. Magnus in love.   Red hair, spectacles, a sharp nose, and a respectable total of years do not prevent a man from falling in love, and so Mr. Magnus, in the full tide of the passion with the port in sight, finds nothing insignificant, but all "a wonder and a wild desire," for he is not really an outside passenger on the Ipswich coach, he is Adam in an Eden that still has the first dew upon it.   Happy Mr. Magnus !—he would serve as well as another for the text of a whole volume.

But it is not he but two of his companions on the journey that must serve as the subjects of this chapter, for they alone are of the right stature.   And they, of course, are the two Wellers : the stout coachman who has just discoursed, with due gravity, on the philosophy of turnpike keeping ; and the perky young man behind, his son, who has just countered one of Mr. Magnus's genial truisms with the remark : "That's what I call a self-evident proposition, as the dog's-meat man said when the housemaid told him he warn't a gentleman."   It is these two philosophers, as English as the beef and beer they carry snugly under their greatcoats. who are beyond

question the two great figures in our comic epic of the
English countryside.   Both are essentially of their time,
their oddest tricks of manner and speech have now passed
away, and yet both are essentially of all time, certainly
of all English history, for they are the English people
from the first Canterbury pilgrims to the latest beanfeast
that went clattering down the road.   Between them
they represent all the English people—that is, all below
the middle classes ; but each has his own section.   Old
Tony Weller, you may say, is the rural member, and
Sam is the city representative.   The two have much in
common, heredity is present in them ; there is a Weller-
ishness (of which they themselves are by no means unaware ; they have a family pride, always due to make
an appearance in any matter of being " gammoned ")
common to both of them, a distinct family likeness ; yet
they are different in character and represent two entirely
different kinds of life.   Old Weller, fat, rubicund,
hoarse and horsey, represents an older tradition ; there is
something rural and earthy in his composition, and his
talk has that dark oracular strain which suggests the great
rustic ; he is not, like Sam, a wit and ironist, but an
immense " character," one of those inscrutable humorists,
oracles of the rural taproom, in whom simplicity and
sophistication seem inextricably tangled, who now appear
supremely foolish and then appear supremely wise, who

are not easily fathomed and understood but are easily
enjoyed, like a poem or a sunset.   Old Weller, we may
say, is Old England.   Sam represents a newer tradition of
the English people ;   he is essentially a product of the
endless streets of the great cities, and particularly the
greatest of them, London, with its colossal tolerance and
good humour and its never-failing irony, a whetstone
for the wits of its poorer citizens.

Although Sam was probably born in the country,
most of his time has been passed in London ; and if his
body did not first make its appearance within sound of
the Bow Bells, his soul certainly belongs to the city, for
he is perhaps the best representative we have of the real
Cockney spirit.   He has the necessary breadth of experience.   " When I wos first pitched neck and crop into
the world, to play at leap-frog with its troubles," he tells
Mr. Pickwick, " I wos a carrier's boy at startin' :   then
a vagginer's, then a helper, then a boots.   Now I 'm a
gen'l'm'n's servant."   He has slept under the arches of
Waterloo Bridge, and knows all the ropes, even the two-
penny ones, the " cheap lodgin'-house, where the beds
is twopence a night."   His father is careful to tell Mr.
Pickwick that Sam's education has not been neglected :
" I took a good deal o' pains with his eddication, sir ;
let him run in the streets when he was wery young, and
shift for his-self.   It 's the only way to make a boy sharp,

sir." From this university Sam has graduated with honours. His knowledge of London is, as we are told, extensive and peculiar. Does Mr. Pickwick require to know where he can obtain a glass of brandy and warm water (to take the taste of Dodson and Fogg out of his mouth), then Sam replies without the slightest hesitation : "Second court on the right-hand side—last house but vun on the same side the vay—take the box as stands in the first fireplace, 'cos there an't no leg in the middle o' the table, wich all the others has, and it 's wery inconvenient." (How fortunate it was for us that they should have chosen this particular tavern, for it is here that old Weller makes his first appearance.) His knowledge of life is equally extensive and peculiar. But his running about in the streets, his numerous and very diverse occupations, his acquaintance with the arches by the river and the doss-houses, have only succeeded in sharpening his wits ; they have hardened his head but not his heart ; so that he provides us with a spectacle new in literature, as Mr. Chesterton has pointed out, namely, that of clever comic servant, whose knowledge of the world is far more extensive than that of his master, but who is not a rascal.

Sam's experience, like that of most genuine philosophers, has taught him to be cynical about the little, unimportant things of this life, such as the conduct of lawyers or the business of voting, but it has left him optimistic about the important things, eating and drinking, travel and adventure, service and love. Like the good Cockney he is, he can see the greater part of life for what it is, a colossal show at which the wise man can stare and laugh, and over which he can nod and wink to other merry philosophers. London has been the greatest of cities for many a year now, and it has probably outlasted the other great capitals of the world, which have worn their bravery of towers and their lace of streets insolently under the stars for a short space and then have been waved back by the gods to the dust : and it has outlasted them probably because it has always been the most tolerant of the great cities. The iron has never entered its soul ; kindness and laughter and a mellow irony have never been entirely banished, with the sunshine, from its maze of dark streets. Its poorer citizens, immured in bricks and mortar as they are, seemingly doomed to the most drab of existences, living often with less than a pavement's width between themselves and utter destitution, have never lost their zest for life and only require a few hours of leisure and a shilling or two to spend to find their way back to Cockaigne. Whoever would learn what harm the modern city can do to the bodies and souls of its inhabitants must not remain in London, but must visit the dark mushroom cities of the provinces, whose grey-faced crowds would often seem to be utterly spiritless and crushed. But that gay ironist, the Cockney, pushing his way about the great show of London, knowing that he is at the heart of things, still moves through a world— a world of unfailing humour, stout and oysters and fried fish, betting and boxing, song and dance and odd figures in bar parlours, and all a jumble of queer streets—that is still the nearest thing we have to the world Dickens knew and to the supernormal world he created for himself.

Sam Weller is the ideal member for Cockneydom. He knows his way about and has so much self-confidence that he can always afford to be waggish and impudent with the world. He is ready for anything, a drink, a kiss, a fight, an adventure, at a moment's notice. The constant irony that is still beloved of the London poor, who as spectators of the staggering show and appalling contrasts of London life must perforce develop into ironic and humorous philosophers, is the very breath of his nostrils. Almost every day in some London street there could be matched such comments as those of his on the electorate of Eatanswill :

"Reg'lar game, sir," replied Mr. Weller ; "our people's a col-lecting down at the Town Arms, and they're a hollering themselves hoarse already."

"Ah," said Mr. Pickwick, "do they seem devoted to their party, Sam ? "

"Never see such dewotion in my life, sir."

"Energetic, eh ? " said Mr. Pickwick.

"Uncommon," replied Sam ; "I never see men eat and drink so much afore. I wonder they an't afeer'd o' bustin'."

"That's the mistaken kindness of the gentry here," said Mr. Pickwick.

"Wery likely," replied Sam, briefly.

Or his remark after hearing the clerks at Dodson and Fogg's discuss their idea of a "capital man of business" :

"Nice men these here, sir, " whispered Mr. Weller to his master ; "wery nice notion of fun they has, sir."

Or even his delectable conversation with the footman at Bath :

"Have you been long in Bath, sir ? " inquired the powdered-headed footman. "I have not had the pleasure of hearing of you before."

"I haven't created any wery surprisin' sensation here, as yet," rejoined Sam, "for me and the other fash'nables only come last night."

"Nice place, sir," said the powdered-headed footman.

"Seems so," observed Sam.

"Pleasant society, sir," remarked the powdered-headed footman. "Very agreeable servants, sir."

"I should think they wos," replied Sam. "Affable, unaffected, say-nothin'-to-nobody sort o' fellers."

"Oh, very much so, indeed, sir," said the powdered-headed footman, taking Sam's remark as a high compliment. "Very much so indeed. Do you do anything in this way, sir ? " inquired the tall footman, producing a small snuff-box with a fox's head on the top of it.

"Not without sneezing," replied Sam.

"Why, it *is* difficult, sir, I confess," said the tall footman. "It may be done by degrees, sir. Coffee is the best practice. I carried coffee, sir, for a long time. It looks very like rappee, sir."

Here a sharp peal at the bell reduced the powdered-headed footman to the ignominious necessity of putting the fox's head in his pocket, and hastening with a humble countenance to Mr. Bantam's "study." By the bye, who ever knew a man who never read or wrote either, who hadn't got some small back parlour which he *would* call a study !

"There is the answer, sir," said the powdered-headed footman. "I am afraid you 'll find it inconveniently large."

"Don't mention it," said Sam, taking a letter with a small enclosure. "It 's just possible as exhausted nature may manage to surwive it."

"I hope we shall meet again, sir," said the powdered-headed footman, rubbing his hands, and following Sam out to the door-step.

"You are wery obligin', sir," replied Sam. "Now, don't allow yourself to be fatigued beyond your powers ; there 's a amiable bein'. Consider what you owe to society, and don't let yourself be injured by too much work. For the sake o' your feller-creeturs, keep yourself as quiet as you can ; only think what a loss you would be ! " With these pathetic words, Sam Weller departed.

"A very singular young man that," said the powdered-headed footman, looking after Mr. Weller, with a countenance which clearly showed he could make nothing of him.

H

—unlike posterity, which has been able to make a great deal of him.

Sam is always a deliberate and conscious humorist, or, perhaps better, wit, and has few if any unconscious absurdities. His set pieces of humour, such as, for example, the tall stories with which he regales his innocent master, seem to me his least interesting passages, though there was a time when I revelled in the story of the pieman and the kittens, or that of the very fat old gentleman and his watch, or that of the melancholy gentleman of principle who ordered in and ate three-shillings'-worth of crumpets and then blew out his brains, and it may well be that I loved them so much as a boy that I contrived to suck out of them then all the marrowy nourishment of humour and finally left them dry bones. Nor—and this is a more serious confession—do I find myself so enthusiastic as most admirers of *Pickwick* over Sam's characteristic allusions and queer similes. Some of them, like that remark about the soldier at the trial, have produced what are by this time classical quotations, and one or two of them, notably that one about the dog's-meat man already quoted, are gems that the memory will wear for ever ; but a great number of them seem to me distinctly forced and not very funny. Indeed, it is as a figure moving through the story and not as the author of comic quotations that Sam Weller is really great. There is hardly anything better in the whole range of Dickens than the relation between him and his master, so productive of rich comedy and yet so profoundly true and, curious as it may sound, so significant ; for once it is admitted that Sam Weller is a worthy representative of the English populace, almost its total history can be deduced from this relation. For Sam is at once extremely disrespectful and extremely devoted ; in short, he is essentially individualistic and independent, like the people of this country, and particularly the poorer people of the great towns ; but, like them too, he frankly admires and supports an aristocratic tradition, knowing "a gen'l'm'n" when he sees one. And as the book proceeds and Mr. Pickwick becomes less and less a silly old fool and more and more a kind of stout English Don Quixote in spectacles and gaiters, so this relation between master and servant deepens As Mr. Chesterton has pointed out, Sam's cheerful knowledge of the world is made to serve his master's still more cheerful ignorance of the world ; the winking ironist of the London streets walks into prison to devote himself to that figure of happy innocence and will not be driven back to liberty.

Old Mr. Weller, as we have already noted, has many characteristics in common with his son, but, though he is a less significant figure in the chronicle, he is perhaps a richer droll. He belongs to a different world, and, with his coach and his country tavern, suggests a background of the countryside just as Sam inevitably calls to mind the London streets.   There is about him a rustic gravity and solemnity in which, however, there gleams an infinity of humour.   Like Sam, he is a philosopher, as the former tells us himself :

" You are quite a philosopher, Sam," said Mr. Pickwick.
" It runs in the family, I b'lieve, sir," replied Mr. Weller.   " My father's wery much in that line, now. If my mother-in-law blows him up, he whistles.   She flies in a passion, and breaks his pipe ; he steps out and gets another.   Then she screams very loud, and falls into 'sterics : and he smokes very comfortably 'til she comes to agin.   That 's philosophy, sir, an't it ? "

It is the height of it, philosophy carried beyond the sphere of mere speculation into that of conduct and there severely tested and emerging in triumph from the ordeal. The core of Mr. Weller's system is, of course, the menace of the widow.   As Sam tells us when we first meet him at the White Hart, if old Mr. Weller had not been offered a marriage licence when he visited Doctors' Commons, after his first wife died and left him four hundred pounds, then he would not have married again and we should not have had the benefit of his profound reasoning on his own experience.   He is essentially a practical philosopher.   We can gather that from his very first speeches, when he and Sam and Mr. Pickwick meet in the tavern :

"Wy, Sammy," said the father, "I han't seen you for two year and better."

"No more you have, old codger," replied the son. "How's mother-in-law?"

"Wy, I'll tell you what, Sammy," said Mr. Weller senior, with much solemnity in his manner ; "there never was a nicer woman as a widder, than that 'ere second wentur o' mine—a sweet creetur she was, Sammy ; all I can say on her now, is, that she was such an uncommon pleasant widder, it's a great pity she ever changed her con-dition. She don't act as a vife, Sammy."

"Don't she, though?" inquired Mr. Weller junior.

The elder Mr. Weller shook his head, as he replied with a sigh, "I've done it once too often, Sammy ; I've done it once too often. Take example by your father, my boy, and be wery careful o' widders all your life, specially if they've kept a public-house, Sammy." Having delivered this parental advice with great pathos, Mr. Weller senior re-filled his pipe from a tin box he carried in his pocket, and, lighting his fresh pipe from the ashes of the old one, commenced smoking at a great rate.

It is soon evident that the old gentleman, like the thinker he is, is capable of transforming a personal and private grievance into something of universal application. Thus he has discovered a sovereign cure for the gout :

"The gout, sir," replied Mr. Weller, "the gout is

a complaint as arises from too much ease and comfort. If ever you 're attacked with the gout, sir, jist you marry a widder as has got a good loud voice, with a decent notion of usin' it, and you 'll never have the gout agin. It 's a capital prescription, sir. I takes it reg'lar, and I can warrant it to drive away any illness as is caused by too much jollity." Having imparted this valuable secret, Mr. Weller drained his glass once more, produced a laboured wink, sighed deeply, and slowly retired.

Nothing could be sounder than his attitude towards that brand of evangelical Christianity, a mixture of tea and toast, pine-apple rum, and flannel waistcoats and moral pocket-handkerchiefs for the infant negroes, patronised by Mrs. Weller. The Shepherd's description of him as " a man of wrath " is really a great compliment, a tribute to his worth as a thinker and his courage as a husband. Not that he is unaware of the limitations of his power ; he is too wise for that, as his reply to Sam clearly shows, when the latter asks why he should allow Mr. Stiggins to show his red nose in the " Marquis of Granby " at all :

Mr. Weller the elder fixed on his son an earnest look, and replied, " 'Cause I 'm a married man, Samivel, 'cause I 'm a married man. When you 're a married man, Samivel, you 'll understand a good many things as you don't understand now ; but vether it 's worth while goin' through so much, to learn so little, as the charity-boy said ven he got to the end of the alphabet, is a matter o' taste. I rayther think it isn't."

Whole volumes on the subject have said less than is contained in this notable rejoinder.

He shares with his son an astonishing mass of curious, out-of-the-way information that gives rise to many sage comments on life. There is, for example, that matter of the poor and their passion for oysters and pickled salmon, a passion that increases with their poverty, which is discussed, for the benefit of Mr. Pickwick, notebook in hand, on the coach going to Ipswich. There is that other matter of turnpike-keepers, who are, it seems, according to old Mr. Weller, "all on 'em men as has met with some disappointment in life. Consequence of vich, they retires from the world, and shuts themselves up in pikes ; partly with the view of being solitary, and partly to rewenge themselves on mankind, by takin' tolls." There is, of course, much in his philosophy that must inevitably appear obscure to a superficial student, and that demands a more profound examination than we can afford to give it in this place. When he and Sammy discuss the valentine, some of his literary judgments are very shrewd indeed, but it seems a pity that so ripe a thinker should have such a horror of poetry :

" 'Tain't in poetry, is it ? " interposed his father.
" No, no," replied Sam.

"Wery glad to hear it," said Mr. Weller. "Poetry's
unnat'ral ; no man ever talked poetry 'cept a beadle on
boxin' day, or Warren's blackin', or Rowland's oil, or
some o' them low fellows ; never let yourself down to
talk poetry, my boy. . . ."

He is probably right in holding that "circumwented"
is a better, though a less tender, word than "circum-
scribed" ; and many good judges will probably join in
demanding "Wot's the good o' callin' a young 'ooman
a Wenus or a angel ? You might jist as well call her a
griffin, or a unicorn, or king's arms at once, which is
wery well known to be a col-lection o' fabulous animals."
Though a richer and riper thinker than his son, he is,
as we might well suppose, less successful as a practical
man. Thus, his recommendation that Mr. Pickwick in
his trial will be well advised to "never mind the character, and stick to the alleybi," though well meant, can
hardly be said to be of much service. His further recom-
mendations that Mr. Pickwick should be smuggled out
of the Fleet either in "a turn-up bedstead" or disguised
as an old woman ; or his later plan, devised by himself
and a friendly cabinetmaker, for removing the old
gentleman in a piano—a very elaborate plot this—

"There ain't no vurks in it. It 'ull hold him easy,
vith his hat and shoes on, and breathe through the legs,
vich his holler. Have a passage ready taken for 'Merriker.

The 'Merrikin gov'ment will never give him up, ven they find as he's got money to spend, Sammy. Let the gov'ner stop there, till Mrs. Bardell's dead, or Mr. Dodson and Fogg's hung (which last ewent I think is the most likely to happen first, Sammy), and then let him come back and write a book about the 'Merrikins as 'll pay all his expenses and more, if he blows 'em up enough "—

though all very ingenious indeed, are more picturesque than useful. Indeed, it is in these legal affairs that Mr. Weller displays his greatest weakness. Those of us who count ourselves among his admirers, both as a man and a philosopher, must deplore his lamentable admiration for Mr. Solomon Pell, that greasy "friend of the Lord Chancellor," and it goes to our heart to see our old friend, backed by a ton or so of fellow-coachmen, gazing with something like awe at this Pell as he drinks his innumerable three-pennyworths of rum. That other weakness of old Mr. Weller's, connected with widows, is, as he says himself, a very different thing, for widows are exceptions to every rule and are equal to at least five-and-twenty ordinary women : it is, in his own words, " a amable weakness," the heel of Achilles, that Mr. Weller shares with other great men, giants of thought or of action, Socrates with his Xanthippe, Napoleon and his Josephine. That which has caused the ruin of empires has laid him low for a season ; but though he could not save himself, he will save others, and so has turned philosopher.

There is no space here in which to comment on all the droll and, occasionally, pathetic actions in which father and son are involved. They are landed in the end, Sam at Mr. Pickwick's house at Dulwich and old Mr. Weller at the public-house near Shooter's Hill (where he was reverenced, very rightly too, as an oracle), at one of those ports of domestic comfort and cosiness at which Dickens loved to land his virtuous characters when he took a final leave of them. We smile at the notion of such epics of the grotesque ending in a ponderous, drowsy Victorian interior, all the white roads of England and all the strange adventures they framed only leading at last to crumpets and horse-hair and heavy Madeira and seven dull neighbours sitting down to saddle-of-mutton ; and yet such was the end of many an actual epic of incredible adventure and endurance, and it was the vision of such comfort and cosiness and dull respectability that led many a man to take a desperate chance on the high seas or at the diggings and sustained him through year after year under brazen and hostile skies. Later, it will be remembered, Dickens resurrected these characters, but the experiment was not a success ; something had been lost, some brightness had fallen from the air ; he was to create individual characters of an equal richness and drollery, but never again could he set them in such an atmosphere as that of *Pickwick*, which was conceived in a mood that could never be captured again, and is, indeed, a May morning of English humour, the Comic Spirit, still young and innocent, suddenly let loose from school.

DICK SWIVELLER

DICK SWIVELLER, like Pistol, is a creature compact of great phrases. But he is more credible, more of a human being and less of a grotesque puppet, than Falstaff's Ancient. At this late date, we can hardly visualise Pistol; he belongs to a vanished world in which London taverns swarmed with rusty, out-at-elbows captains, with tall swords and even taller phrases, lean, hungry rats who always appeared to be passing swiftly through a little space of ease and inaction between two wars, two epics, but who, in truth, finding the taverns more agreeable than the camps, usually contrived to avoid any actual campaigns and lived as bullies and parasites rather than as soldiers. The type was so familiar that it was recognised as soon as the long sword and the long moustachios made their appearance, and Pistol was merely a supremely comic specimen of it. But now, though his astonishing phrases, those purple patches he clipped from the tragedians, the very cloak and dagger of speech, are securely lodged (and, I hope, freely entertained) in our memories, Pistol himself is nothing but a figure fading out of some old tapestry. Swiveller, on the other hand, is a creature of our own time. His hat and coat, his tricks of speech, his songs and his tipple, may all belong to the day before yesterday ; but Swiveller himself still exists and may be lolling on a high stool (no mean accomplishment) at the " General Office " round the corner : we have sadly wasted our time if we have never met him. It would be better to use the plural and say that the Swivellers, the family, the type, still exist. They have not that greatness of phrase which distinguishes Dick, their representative in letters, but they have the same characteristics, and Dick is only the essence of them, winged about, as no essence was ever winged before, with great words.

When young people are sufficiently imaginative to appreciate art but not imaginative enough to create it, when they are buried in sophistication and yet still wanting in experience, they generally pass through a period in which life seems less than nothing if it is not eked out with art. This does not mean merely that art is necessary to their lives, that their imagination must have its rich, sustaining food : it means that their existence itself must be somehow pressed into the patterns of art, that their actions, gestures, and speech must take on a likeness to the actions, gestures, and speech that they have come to know in admired works of art, in poetry,

fiction, and the drama. They have not sufficient imagination to turn life into art, to remark the epic, the tragedy,
and the comedy, lurking somewhere in the common stuff
of existence ; but they have sufficient imagination to
turn art into life, to play at being a figure in an epic or
a tragedy (but not a comedy, for then they would really
see themselves and their attitudes would collapse) and
transfigure their surroundings and disguise the persons
they meet with the aid of coloured lights and hidden
orchestras sounding themes of doom. This is the period
of high-falutin. Girls, like Jane Austen's Catherine
Morland, move like somnambulists through the most
prosaic scenes as the heroines of wild romance. Serious
young men wrap themselves in Byronic gloom and pace
the dark streets enjoying their utter despair. But there
are some young men, who happen to have imagination
but also a lively sense of the ludicrous, who walk into this
maze but never leave go of the silken thread of common-
sense, so that while they enjoy their romantic play-acting,
relishing the large gestures and the tremendous speeches,
they also contrive to enjoy the absurdity of it all, knowing
very well that they are play-acting. Thus they are
walking parodies of art. A good parody is the product
of a double enjoyment, for the parodist has really enjoyed
imitating the good things, the music, the resounding
phrase, and so forth, in a writer, while he has also en-

joyed letting his sense of humour play over the bad things
that he has exaggerated and so emphasised. Thus it is
that our friend Swiveller, who is undoubtedly one of the
lively young men mentioned above, enjoys his high-falutin,
smacks his lips over his magnificent phrases, but knows
very well that he is absurd and enjoys that fact too. The
only difference is that Swiveller is not deliberate, like the
parodist ; he has just drifted into his happy condition
just as he has drifted into debt.

When we first meet him, Dick Swiveller is existing
precariously in a room above a tobacconist's shop (you
had only to step out on to the staircase and sniff heartily
to save yourself the cost of many a pinch of snuff) near
Drury Lane. Although he always takes care to speak
of his rooms or lodgings or chambers, he is actually the
tenant of a small single apartment, in which the only
object of interest is a bedstead that looks like a bookcase
and, indeed, has to be regarded as a bookcase by any
visitor who wishes to be considered a friend. His
finances are in a deplorable state. Indeed, he owes
money in all directions and is gradually closing down
whole sections of the town because he is in debt to so
many of the neighbouring shops. This we know from
his own account of the matter :

" I enter in this little book the names of the streest
that I can't go down while the shops are open. This

dinner to-day closes Long Acre. I bought a pair of
boots in Great Queen Street last week, and made that
no thoroughfare too. There's only one avenue to the
Strand left open now, and I shall have to stop up that
to-night with a pair of gloves. The roads are closing
so fast in every direction, that in about a month's time,
unless my aunt sends me a remittance, I shall have to go
three or four miles out of town to get over the way."

Never were finance and topography so quaintly wedded.
He sees the lady of his choice, Miss Sophy Wackles,
accept the hand and heart of one Cheggs, a market
gardener, a creature from the outer darkness. Later,
he enters the office of Sampson Brass and there is entombed, so far as it is possible for so mercurial a soul to
be entombed, for weeks and months on end, until at last
he takes to his bed with a raging fever, to be nursed by
his curious little friend, the Marchioness. Here, it is
evident, is very poor material for a care-free, happy
existence ; this is not the stuff out of which a romantic
and poetical life can be fashioned ; and yet Dick, a
romantic and poetical soul, contrives to be happy. Indeed,
he is probably the happiest figure in the whole book.

He contrives to enjoy himself by indulging, without
stint, his literary sense. If he cannot have the romantic
trappings, the poetical action, he can, and does, have the
language. He feasts sumptuously on rich quotations.
Gorgeous phrases clothe him in silks and velvet. He is

wafted where he will, far above dull reality, far beyond the clutch of circumstance, on the wings of metaphor. Noble adjectives wait upon him, the lord of language. This passion for words, marvellous in themselves and miraculous in felicitous arrangement, is the mark of the literary sense and the very soul of literature, and Dick Swiveller, like one of the few comic characters in recent fiction that have real vitality, Mr. Polly, and unlike so many modern critics, who can appreciate ideas but have no interest in or enjoyment of expression, the power of the word, and are therefore shut off from literature, talk of it as they will, has the literary sense in no common degree and so contrives to turn his daily existence into a kind of wild literature that he reads and enjoys as it passes. It is true that he is fortified against anxiety and depression by one of those happy-go-lucky temperaments that can forget all their troubles over a glass, a song, and a chat with a friend. But that is not his secret. A glass of cold gin and water would always help him to put trouble and care on one side for the moment, but when he can call it, as he does, "the rosy wine," and can tell his companion (who is using the same tumbler) to "fan the sinking flame of hilarity with the wing of friendship," he is something more than merely forgetful of misery, he is definitely happy, intoxicated not so much by the gin he is drinking as by the phrases he is making.

He moves happily in a mist, not of alcohol, but of romance and art. "What is the odds," he remarks in one place, referring, it must be confessed, to the fact that he had been extremely drunk on the previous evening, "what is the odds so long as the fire of soul is kindled at the taper of conwiviality, and the wing of friendship never moults a feather!" And what are a headache and an empty purse when here to hand are such glorious draughts of metaphor, such shining heaps of newly minted phrases?

That convivial circle, the "Glorious Apollers," were wise in electing our friend Swiveller as Perpetual Grand Master. They were wise not only because he is the soul of convivial oratory and song, pledged to see that the wing of friendship "is not clipped but expanded and serene," in short, the very man for the chair, but for a deeper reason, because he is one of those choice spirits who serve Apollo himself and are sustained by him. Never does Mr. Swiveller speak without paying, indirectly, homage to the radiant tuneful god. Never does he quit what he calls "the gay and festive scene and halls of dazzling light" without sacrificing a heap of metaphors to the deity, who must have blessed, with winged words and unfailing melody, any convivial circle presided over by Mr. Swiveller. What could be better than the fraternal greeting between him and Mr. Chuckster, another Glorious Apollo:

"Won't you come in?" said Dick. "All alone. Swiveller solus. ''Tis now the witching——'"

"'Hour of night!'"

"'When churchyards yawn.'"

"'And graves give up their dead.'"

At the end of this quotation in dialogue, each gentleman struck an attitude, and immediately subsiding into prose walked into the office. Such morsels of enthusiasm are common among the Glorious Apollos, and were indeed the links that bound them together, and raised them above the cold dull earth.

Who that has known shabby young clerks, spirited souls caught in a web of routine, immured as they are in dungeons of brick, mortar, and ledgers, has not seen them indulge in such antics, rushing for a second or so into some mad world of romance, an Aldebaran's distance from their double-entry, discovering a kind of safety-valve in such wistful absurdities? Did not Mr. Swiveller and Mr. Chuckster, after thus greeting one another and then finding that each was in good health, "in compliance with a solemn custom of the ancient Brotherhood to which they belonged," then join in a fragment of the duet, "All 's well," with a long shake at the end? And having thus relieved their feelings, all *is* well with them: desperate as their condition is, wedged tight as they are in the dullest and bleakest prose of life, they can yet break through to give their souls a breath of poetry: they have been saved by their tutelary god, Apollo.

The advantage of having such a temperament as Dick Swiveller's is that situations that would be either foolish or painful to ordinary persons are nothing less than meat and drink to your romantic self. Thus the affair of Sophy Wackles is a godsend to Swiveller. Around this lost love (who would have accepted him quickly enough if he had offered himself) most of his imperishable phrases are heaped. There is nothing richer in the whole book than his parting dialogue, in which he rapturously assumes the part of an injured swain, with the fickle Sophy :

Near the door sat Miss Sophy, still fluttered and confused by the attentions of Mr. Cheggs, and by her side Richard Swiveller lingered, for a moment to exchange a few parting words.

"My boat is on the shore and my bark is on the sea, but before I pass this door I will say farewell to thee," murmured Dick, looking gloomily upon her.

"Are you going ? " said Miss Sophy, whose heart sunk within her at the result of her stratagem, but who affected a light indifference notwithstanding.

"Am I going ! " echoed Dick bitterly. "Yes, I am. What then ? "

"Nothing, except that it's very early," said Miss Sophy, "but you are your own master of course."

"I would that I had been my own mistress too," said Dick, "before I had ever entertained a thought of you. Miss Wackles, I believed you true, and I was blest in so believing, but now I mourn that e'er I knew, a girl so fair yet so deceiving."

Miss Sophy bit her lip and affected to look with great interest after Mr. Cheggs, who was quaffing lemonade in the distance.

"I came here," said Dick, rather oblivious of the purpose with which he had really come, "with my bosom expanded, my heart dilated, and my sentiments of a corresponding description. I go away with feelings that may be conceived, but cannot be described : feeling within myself the desolating truth that my best affections have experienced, this night, a stifler !

"I am sure I don't know what you mean, Mr. Swiveller," said Miss Sophy with downcast eyes. " I 'm very sorry if——"

"Sorry, ma'am !" said Dick, "sorry in the possession of a Cheggs ! . . ."

Secure in such an abyss of disillusion, he is now completely happy. Like a good many more serious persons, he can wring more pleasure out of the idea of a Sophy lost to him for ever than he ever could have wrung out of the girl's actual company. Unreciprocated love is a theme for which he has an abundant store of apt quotations and very original and very moving phrases, and later, whenever we discover him in his cups or otherwise expansive, though by this time he has probably forgotten everything about the girl, he makes some reference to the lost Sophy, now plighted to her market gardener. When Quilp, that convivial horror, demands from Dick the name of some beauty for a toast, we are not surprised

when Sophy is immediately named.   But what bitterness,
what despair, unfathomable, is suggested when that name
is mentioned : " a Being of brightness and beauty will
be offered up a sacrifice at Cheggs' altar " ; and later
the same sacrificial metaphor is introduced again, for we
are told that Sophy is " immolating herself upon the
shrine of Cheggs." The emphasis upon the name of
the fortunate suitor is significant, and suggests that our
Glorious Apollo, his literary instinct repelled, would
forgive the girl her imaginary renunciation of him if only
she had not chosen a Cheggs.   The literary artist in him,
a thorough romantic, appears to be incensed mainly by
the thought that " Cheggs " is to be perpetuated.   And
long after this scene with Quilp, indeed immediately after
he has been playing cribbage with the Marchioness, he
returns to the matter, but by this time his mood has
changed, the bitterness has almost gone, and he speaks,
sternly yet with a touch of wistfulness, as one who has
outstared the Gorgon-face of this life's tragedy and can
but mutely wave a hand of pity towards the failures,
stricken in stone, he passes by the way :

" These rubbers," said Mr. Swiveller, putting on his
nightcap in exactly the same style as he wore his hat,
" remind me of the matrimonial fireside. Cheggs'
wife plays cribbage ; all-fours likewise. She rings the
changes on 'em now. From sport to sport they hurry

her, to banish her regrets, and when they win a smile from her they think that she forgets—but she don't. By this time, I should say," added Richard, getting his left cheek into profile, and looking complacently at the reflection of a very little scrap of whisker in the looking-glass ; " by this time, I should say, the iron has entered into her soul. It serves her right."

We can almost catch a glimpse of poor Sophy looking out over a dreary sea of Cheggs, while in the far distance the happy isles of Swiveller, a mist of gold upon the horizon, pale and recede and utterly vanish.

It was the opinion of both Mr. Sampson Brass and Miss Sally Brass that Dick Swiveller had mistaken his calling and would never make a lawyer, no, not if he lived a thousand years. They were driven to this conclusion, which we share, because Dick proved uncommonly slow when Mr. Brass hinted that the strange lodger, then engaged in his twenty-six hours' sleep, might have said that he wished his property on the premises to fall to Mr. Brass if anything should happen to him. Dick, who knew no more than Apollo himself of these little sharp practices, proved on this occasion to have an inconveniently clear memory But he also proved that a young gentleman of courage, address, and imagination has his uses in the world. After the new lodger had been asleep six-and-twenty hours and every effort had been made to waken him accidentally, including

frequent double-knocks at the street door, the moving
of chests of drawers on the floor above, and instructions
to the little maid-servant to fall downstairs every now
and then, all to no purpose, it was Swiveller who battered
the upper panels of the door with a large ruler and thus
succeeded in rousing the sleeper, and it was he who faced
the angry man when the Sampsons had fled. Not only
did he stand his ground, but he dealt with the whole
situation, a very unusual one, manfully, and contrived to
rebuke this glutton of unconsciousness :

" . . . We have been distracted with fears that you
were dead, sir," said Dick, gently sliding to the ground,
" and the short and the long of it is, that we cannot allow
single gentlemen to come into this establishment and
sleep like double gentlemen without paying extra for it."
    " Indeed ! " cried the lodger.
    " Yes, sir, indeed," returned Dick, yielding to his
destiny and saying whatever came uppermost ; " an
equal quantity of slumber was never got out of one bed,
and if you 're going to sleep in that way, you must pay
for a double-bedded room."

The matter in a nutshell.

No matter how we straddle and gesticulate, light our
coloured fires, and bid the toy trumpets sound from the
mimic battlements, no matter, in short, how we play at
romance, it frequently happens that when real romance
has come to us, it has stolen in unobserved while we have

been at our play. Mr. Swiveller, who could be romantic about anything and everything, began his acquaintance with Sally Brass's little half-starved drudge, the tiny maid who lived like a mole out of sight, and is known to us now, thanks to our friend's whimsical invention, as the Marchioness, in a mood of idle good-humour. Finding that she looked through the office key-hole when he was alone there (" for company "), he joined the queer little creature downstairs, treated her to a plate of bread and beef and a hot drink, of which she was sadly in need, and taught her to play cribbage. She was not much of an audience, being entirely ignorant of everything that passed outside the house just as she missed nothing, not a look nor a syllable, of what went forward inside the house, but she would do, and Dick gave her a taste of what a Glorious Apollo could be like in his hours of slippered ease. They make a quaint pair, sitting down to cribbage in the gloomy basement ; the fantastic clerk, with his battered hat still perched on the side of his head, and his aquatic jacket with the tight sleeves ; and the under-sized drudge, as sharp-featured as a little mouse, in her odds and ends of tattered garments, her appetite satisfied for once, fiercely concentrating on the new delight of cards, and somewhat alarmed by the strange gestures and speech of the visiting god, now full of warm liquor and nonsense :

"With which object in view, Marchioness," said Mr. Swiveller gravely, "I shall ask your ladyship's permission to put the board in my pocket, and to retire from the presence when I have finished this tankard ; merely observing, Marchioness, that since life like a river is flowing, I care not how fast it rolls on, ma'am, on, while such purl on the bank still is growing, and such eyes light the waves as they run. Marchioness, your health. You will excuse my wearing my hat, but the palace is damp, and the marble floor is—if I may be allowed the expression—sloppy."

As a precaution against this latter inconvenience, Mr. Swiveller had been sitting for some time with his feet on the hob, in which attitude he now gave utterance to these apologetic observations, and slowly sipped the last choice drops of nectar.

"The Baron Sampsono Brasso and his fair sister are (you tell me) at the Play ? " said Mr. Swiveller, leaning his left arm heavily upon the table, and raising his voice and his right leg after the manner of a theatrical bandit.

The Marchioness nodded.

"Ha ! " said Mr. Swiveller, with a portentous frown. "'Tis well. Marchioness !—but no matter. Some wine there. Ho ! " He illustrated these melodramatic morsels, by handing the tankard to himself with great humility, receiving it haughtily, drinking from it thirstily, and smacking his lips fiercely. . . .

Mr. Swiveller retires that night to meditate for a moment or so upon his lost Sophy and then to play on his flute, very slowly and very badly, the air " Away with melancholy," for several hours in bed. But his romance has already begun. There is perhaps no more solid and satisfactory love story in all Dickens than the affair of Dick Swiveller and his Marchioness. It has practically all the elements and dramatic movement necessary to a good love story. It begins with a casual act of kindness, when the male steps down like a god to the astonished and delighted female, who is still in her grub stage. This is more than repaid, during the time when Dick is delirious with fever and is nursed by the Marchioness, by that fierce feminine devotion which makes all possible masculine attentions seem merely casual and selfish. Then, after the Kit episode is rounded off and Dick comes into his annuity, it is his turn again, and he sends her to school for six years, during which time she passes from grub to chrysalis and finally wings her way out into the sunshine. The last scene is their cottage (with a smoking-box) at Hampstead, a happy marriage. That is our idea of a satisfactory love story, and perhaps it helps to compensate us, in spite of its earlier date, for Toots' loss of Florence Dombey, a black business, as Toots is, without a doubt, the greatest lover in Dickens.

We do not know what Mr. Swiveller did with himself on his retirement to Hampstead, beyond the fact that he ruminated in the smoking-box, played cribbage with his wife, and occasionally entertained his fellow Apollo, Mr. Chuckster. But we are told that when the

Marchioness was at school, the governor of the establishment, to which he paid a monthly visit, "looked upon him as a literary gentleman of eccentric habits, and of a most prodigious talent in quotation." That he had the literary sense, the poet's passion for and delight in words, we know already, but this opinion of the governor's affords us a clue to what he did with himself at Hampstead. He wrote. The form his writing chose to honour is matter for conjecture ; but when we remember our friend's love of the theatre, his native touch of the histrionic, we must admit that it is more than likely that he wrote plays, tremendous things, full of the fire of soul, in five deeply tragic acts. There may come a day when one of us, rummaging in the threepenny box, will come upon : " Gonzalo : Or the Brigand's Vengeance. A Tragedy. By Richard Swiveller." It will be dedicated to the Marchioness.

MR. MICAWBER

IT is odd to think of the sinister Mr. Murdstone as the tool of Providence, acting unwittingly as its compensating finger, restoring the balance in the affairs of poor little Copperfield. But that is what he was. The ten-year-old David is immured in Murdstone and Grinby's warehouse, with its dirt and decaying floors and scuffling old grey rats. But he must have lodgings, cheap lodgings, and so Mr. Murdstone bethinks himself of a certain not very successful agent of the firm who has a room to let in Windsor Terrace, City Road, and decides that David shall go there. David is taken into the counting-house and introduced to his new landlord :

" A stoutish, middle-aged person, in a brown surtout and black tights and shoes, with no more hair upon his head (which was a large one, and very shining) than there is upon an egg, and with a very extensive face, which he turned full upon me. His clothes were shabby, but he had an imposing shirt-collar on. He carried a jaunty sort of stick, with a large pair of rusty tassels to it ; and a quizzing-glass hung outside his coat, —for ornament, I afterwards found, as he very seldom looked through it, and couldn't see anything when he did. . . .

It is Mr. Micawber, the inimitable, the unique Mr. Micawber. Henceforward, we know that once our bottle-washing and label-pasting is done, in that dark warehouse at Blackfriars, there will be this god-like creature waiting for us at home ; and that when Murdstone and Grinby's is nothing more than an evil memory and we have almost forgotten Windsor Terrace, City Road, we have not yet done with the great Micawber, who will continue to pop up in odd places and send us letters when we are least expecting them, letters that are worth more than all the money he will contrive to borrow from us from time to time ; and in short—as the great man himself would say—an account has been opened for us in the Bank of Humour where we have been given unlimited credit. Our whole existence has been enriched by the flavour of Micawber so that it can never taste quite the same again, can never be entirely flat and saltless whatever may happen to us. Little did Mr. Murdstone imagine that by an idle choice of a landlord he was to wipe off all our scores against him and actually leave us in his debt. Micawber has arrived, and the balance has been more than restored. Perhaps this is the only occasion in the life of that hard-pressed gentleman on which he and a credit balance have arrived together.

Mr. Micawber is unquestionably the greatest of all Dickens' comic figures. Unlike so many of the others, he is droll both in character and in speech ; he would be vastly entertaining if he were only described to us, if we were only allowed to see him from a distance and never met him face to face or heard him speak ; the idea of him is comic ; but in addition to that, of course, he is infinitely droll in speech, always saying the kind of thing we expect him to say but always saying it better, being more himself, so to speak, every time we meet him, as such persons are in real life. He is not only the greatest of Dickens' comic figures, but, with the one exception of Falstaff, he is the greatest comic figure in the whole range of English literature, a literature supremely rich in such characters. Falstaff is greater because he is himself a comic genius ; in him the two familiar types of characters, the comic rogue and the comic butt, are combined, for he is a comic rogue who is his own butt, and as such he is unique. To this must be added his extraordinary versatility, the teeming abundance of his wit and humour, ranging from crude horse-play to a kind of comic philosophy, which is only displayed within a comparatively small compass (and perhaps necessarily so, for no man, not even a Shakespeare, could have kept the Falstaff of *Henry the Fourth*, part 1, going long—only a god could have fed the furnace of that wit) but makes him tower above any other comic character. Micawber must be included in quite another category, namely, that of the great solemn fools, who do not offer us their wit and humour but only themselves, who do not make jokes but are themselves one endless joke. If Micawber —and all the persons of his kind (and most of us have known a few)—should realise even for a moment that he is funny, he would be ruined for us ; but happily he does not, and while we are actually in his presence—and what a presence—we too must be as solemn as he is, the greatest of all the great solemn fools. It is only when his majesty has departed that we can break into inextinguishable laughter.

The story that Micawber adorns is different from the other Dickens novels in having a certain autobiographical basis : Dickens is making direct use of a number of his own childish experiences. There strolled magnificently through all the memories of his childhood and youth one extraordinary figure, his father, John Dickens, and it was he who became Mr. Micawber. So close at times are the two, the " Prodigal Father " (as Dickens called him) and the great comic character, that the description of Micawber sitting in state with his petition to the King in the Marshalsea, at the end of the eleventh chapter, is taken almost word for word from his own autobiographical notes describing an identical scene in the Marshalsea in which his father figured prominently. Thus we can say that in the creation of this monument of humour, Nature herself laid the foundations and was responsible for the general lines of the structure, while Dickens simply added the decoration, those touches of art necessary when cold print has to take the place of warm breathing reality. It is more than likely that all the most successful characters of fiction and drama are created in this way; they are neither elaborate pieces of portrait painting, on the one hand, nor examples of pure creation, creatures dropped from the blue, on the other; but, if they are comic characters, have their origin in persons long known and humorously and lovingly observed, pondered over, rolled—as it were—on the author's palate until he has the very flavour of them, and then subtly transformed by art, the non-essential parts pared away and the essential coloured and heightened, until at last we have characters who, in a short acquaintance begun and ended in a few chapters, have the same effect upon us that their originals would have in real life if we had known them for years. It is a pity that we have not chapter and verse for this creative process, the real person and the fictitious one side by side, so that we could actually observe the transformation.

Comic figures created in this fashion seize hold of our imagination so strongly because not only have they the

wild absurdity that a humorous and fanciful author, like
Dickens, can give to the speech of his figures, they have
also a certain solidity, a psychological richness, that sets
them far above those brittle creatures who, like so many
of Dickens' later characters, are simply an eccentric trick
of speech and gesture and nothing more, characters that
have no insides but are merely masks, clothes, and wires.
Thus Micawber, in his talk, has all the wild absurdity
of a comic individual, and particularly, of course, a comic
Dickens individual, and he has too the psychological
richness and solidity of a universal type and is therefore,
unlike so many entertaining characters, a fruitful theme
for any man's discourse. Volumes passing a score of
philosophies under review could be written on the
Micawbers.

Really great absurdities of speech are like really great
passages of poetry, they cannot be analysed any more than
a scent can be analysed ; they are simply miraculous
assemblages of words. Why they should be so ridiculous
is, and must remain, a mystery. Faced with them, we
can only enjoy and give thanks, taking our analysis elsewhere. In the last resort, speech and character cannot, of
course, be separated, one being the expression of the other,
and concerning Mr. Micawber's character there is a great
deal to be said, so that his delicious conversation, which
in its highest flights of absurdity, as we have seen, is

beyond analysis, can be very briefly examined in passing. Its most obvious characteristic is its trick of anti-climax. Mr. Micawber indulges in a very florid and theatrical rhetoric that always breaks down ; just when his fantastic bark appears to be safely launched on the flood of oratory, we hear the grating of the keel and discover that he has run aground ; his habit of giving everything a false dignity in his talk (which perhaps reaches its climax in his reference to the man from the waterworks as a " Minion of Power "), as if he were not an impecunious commercial traveller chatting with his friends but a statesman addressing the senate of some vast empire, is ridiculous enough, but it is made still more ridiculous by the fact that he cannot keep it up, his invention or his vocabulary not being equal to the demand, so that he inevitably flounders and breaks down. But a further touch of absurdity is added by the fact that though—so to speak—the matter breaks down, the manner does not : we can realise that at the moment when his oratory is crashing down into the commonplace, his pompousness is becoming even more marked, that " certain conde-scending roll in his voice " and that " certain indescribable air of doing something genteel " being more noticeable than ever. Nothing, we imagine, that he ever says can be delivered with such a dignified and genteel air as that " In short " which always arrives when his first gushing stream of oratory is drying up and he is casting about—usually in vain—for other springs of noble and resounding speech. We have only to take a single scene, let us say that in which he says good-bye to David before leaving for Plymouth in the earlier part of the book, to discover several excellent examples of this oratorical anti-climax and bathos. Mr. Micawber, with his capital histrionic sense, is aware of the solemnity of the occasion and is in a rather mournfully didactic mood "Procrastination," he remarks to David, "is the thief of time. Collar him." Touching on Mrs. Micawber's father, who has been hurled into the conversation by Mrs. Micawber, he observes : "Take him for all in all, we ne'er shall—in short, make the acquaintance, probably, of anybody else possessing, at his time of life, the same legs for gaiters, and able to read the same description of print, without spectacles." And then later when he gives us his great contribution to economics and ethics : " Annual income twenty pounds, annual expenditure nineteen nineteen six, result happiness. Annual income twenty pounds, annual expenditure twenty pounds ought and six, result misery. The blossom is blighted, the leaf is withered, the God of Day goes down upon the dreary scene, and—in short, you are for ever floored. As I am." And when he had said this, we are told, Mr. Micawber drank a glass of punch with an air of great enjoyment and satisfaction, and whistled the College Hornpipe. And well he might, for, having expressed the misery of his position in what he considers such excellent rhetoric (for he himself soars high above bathos), he is perfectly happy, for he is an orator, an artist ; he has the so-called " artistic temperament," and is indeed perhaps our very best example of it.

It is significant, however, that Mr. Micawber is not an artist by profession but a commercial gentleman. But just as many artists, perhaps the majority of them, have not even a glimmer of the artistic temperament, so many gentlemen engaged in business, particularly in its vaguer and looser forms, on its fringes, in dubious agencies and so forth, are, like Micawber, almost perfect specimens of the temperament. One of the greatest and most astonishing Bohemians I have ever met was a certain dissipated watchmaker of the town of Maidstone in Kent. It is on the lounging and strange borderlands of trade, where blossom for a season the odd little companies in odd little towns, that our Micawbers are to be encountered. " The truly gorgeous and great personality," Mr. Chesterton remarks very rightly, " he who talks as no one else could talk and feels with an elementary fire, you will never find this man on any cabinet bench, in any literary circle, at any society dinner. Least of all will you find him in artistic society ; he is utterly unknown in Bohemia." No, he is tucked away in the general office of the Bristol Leatherworks, or may be found in East Lancashire, acting as the local representative of the Imperial Patent Mat Company. In such places, behind a door in some dingy provincial street, unhonoured and unsung, are our Micawbers, personalities like sunsets, and we are unfortunate, to say the least of it, if we have not known at least one of them.

Too much has been made of Mr. Micawber's mere hopefulness : the phrase about "waiting for something to turn up" seems almost to have hypnotised everybody. Not that he was not supremely hopeful, one of the ripest of optimists, but he cannot be explained merely in terms of optimism : the analysis must be carried much further. His temperament is, of course, extremely elastic ; his moods are like quicksilver, and much of his drollery arises from his astonishingly rapid changes from the very depths of despair to the height of gaiety and good-fellow-ship. When creditors, dirty-faced men for the most part, called at his house and shouted "Swindlers" and "Robbers" up the stairs, Mr. Micawber, it will be remembered, "would be transported with grief and mortification, even to the length (as I was once made aware by a scream from his wife) of making motions at himself with a razor ; but within half an hour afterwards, he would polish up his shoes with extraordinary pains, and go out, humming a tune with a greater air of gentility

than ever." And when little David visited him in the
Marshalsea, Mr. Micawber wept and solemnly conjured
his youthful visitor to take warning by his fate, but then
immediately afterwards borrowed a shilling, sent out for
some porter, sat down to his room-mate's loin of mutton,
and was his glorious self again. He positively juggles
with his moods, and can touch the extremes within the
space of a single sentence. One of the most amusing,
though by no means one of the quickest, of his changes
is that at Canterbury when he and David meet for the
first time since the early days in London. The three of
them (for Mrs. Micawber is there—seeing the Medway)
sit down to fish, roast veal, fried sausage-meat, partridge,
and pudding, wine, strong ale and, after dinner, a bowl
of hot punch ; the evening is decidedly festive, healths
are drunk all round, Mr. Micawber delivers an eulogium
on the character of Mrs. Micawber (as well he might),
and they end by singing " Auld Lang Syne " and " Here 's
a hand, my trusty frere "—Mr. Micawber throughout
being the very picture of conviviality and high spirits.
Yet David receives the following letter, early the next
morning, a letter clearly written within quarter of an
hour after his departure the previous night :

My Dear Young Friend,
    The die is cast—all is over. Hiding the ravages of
care with a sickly mask of mirth, I have not informed

you, this evening, that there is no hope of the remittance !
Under these circumstances, alike humiliating to con-
template, and humiliating to relate, I have discharged
the pecuniary liability contracted at this establishment,
by giving a note of hand, made payable fourteen days after
date, at my residence, Pentonville, London. When it
becomes due, it will not be taken up. The result is destruction. The bolt is impending, and the tree must fall.

Let the wretched man who now addresses you, my
dear Copperfield, be a beacon to you through life. He
writes with that intention, and in that hope. If he could
think himself of so much use, one gleam of day might,
by possibility, penetrate into the cheerless dungeon of his
remaining existence—though his longevity is, at present
(to say the least of it), extremely problematical.

This is the last communication, my dear Copperfield,
you will ever receive

From

The

Beggared Outcast,

WILKINS MICAWBER.

On receipt of this startling communication, David immediately runs to the hotel in the hope of being able to
comfort his friend, but on the way there he meets the
London coach—" with Mr. and Mrs. Micawber up
behind ; Mr. Micawber, the very picture of tranquil
enjoyment, smiling at Mrs. Micawber's conversation,
eating walnuts out of a paper bag, with a bottle sticking
out of his breast-pocket." The Beggared Outcast had
promptly vanished once he had written that heart-rending

letter, and his place had been probably taken at once by Mr. Micawber the genteel man of the world and, for the nonce, the complacent author.

The secret of Mr. Micawber is that he does not really live in this world at all : he lives in a world of his own. It is a world in which he himself is clearly a man of talent, for whom great prizes are waiting round the next corner, where an I O U clearly set out and given to the proper person or an entry in a little notebook is as good as cash down, where everything is larger and simpler and richer and more romantic than the things of this world. In short—to echo him once more—he lives entirely in his imagination : he has the real artistic temperament. Let circumstances cast him down ever so little, then he cries farewell and plunges headlong into the dark gulf of despair ; but within a short space of time he has not only climbed out of that gulf into the common daylight of ordinary cheerfulness, he has soared away into the very empyrean of human happiness : he will have no half-measures in his moods, because a robust, romantic, and (to speak truth) somewhat theatrical imagination takes no delight in half-measures ; it demands either the green limelight and the muted strings or every light in the house ablaze and the full orchestra crashing in triumph. But the real world, observing that Wilkins Micawber will not consent to live in it, plans a hearty revenge. It contrives

that the said Micawber shall be for ever in difficulties ;
that his talent shall pass unrecognised (except by Mrs.
Micawber) and his offers—as she herself tells us—
received with contumely ; that neither corn nor coals
shall sustain him, and that he shall be for ever head over
ears in debt, existing in a wilderness of notes of hand,
discounted bills, and I O U's ; and so, eternally jostled
by creditors and bailiffs, in and out of the debtors' prison,
exchanging one set of miserable lodgings for another,
pawning the few remaining possessions in order to pay
for the next meal, he and his wife and their ever-increasing
family are for ever driven from pillar to post, can never
breathe freely, clear themselves, settle down as decent
citizens willing and able to look any man in the face ;
and thus would seem to be in a truly wretched condition.
Short of actual crime—and borrowing on such a scale
appears to be dangerously near a criminal proceeding—it
is hardly possible to imagine an existence more squalid,
uncomfortable, and hopeless.   This world, it would seem,
has revenged itself very thoroughly.

But actually it has done nothing of the kind, for Mr.
Micawber remains unscathed, living as he does in some
other world of his own.   The above account of his way
of life is true enough as it is glimpsed from the real world ;
but Mr. Micawber himself does not really see it like this,
as we may gather from his talk, nor does his wife, nor,

indeed, does any one who is under the spell of his glamour-
ous imagination and walks with him for a space in his
own private Eden.   If a man who has just been quarrel-
ling with the turncock from the waterworks can dismiss
the matter with a reference to " the momentary laceration
of a wounded spirit, made sensitive by a recent collision
with the Minion of Power," he is beyond the corroding
touch of bitter circumstance ; the slings and arrows of
outrageous fortune whistle by, leaving him unhurt ;
his imagination has provided him with one of those fairy
cloaks that enable their wearers to brave all dangers.
Mr. Micawber sees himself as the central figure in some
colossal wild romance, to which even the most disastrous
events do but add an intensely absorbing and moving
chapter or so and call for nobler attitudes and more
magnificent rhetoric on the part of the principal actor.
Once things are seen in that romantic haze, so that they
loom splendid or sinister and run riot in scarlet and black
and gold, the dreariness, the hopelessness, of the petty
tale that is the world's report of Mr. Micawber's life
completely disappear : he goes his way to the sound of
epic drums, the trumpets of tragedy, and the flutes and
violins of romance.   To him, the present is always a
crisis, whether of good or ill fortune matters not, a crisis
to be enjoyed as the latest and strangest scene in the
drama ; the past, far from being a hopeless record from

which remembrance turns her face, is an Othello's tale of battles, sieges, fortunes, of moving accidents by flood and field, of hairbreadth 'scapes i' the imminent deadly breach ; the future, shining round the next corner, is a happy ending.

What chance has poverty, with its poor shifts and wretched limitations, its dinginess and drabness, with a mind so wedded to high romance, so intoxicated with opulent images and phrases, so richly nourished by the milk and honey of words ? What does it matter what facts have to be faced if they are first sent to the carnival of the romantic imagination and so always return the strangest and most fascinating company, still moving to music in their tragic and comic masks ? David was a poor little fellow of ten, a timid little washer of bottles, when he lodged, dingily and precariously like a mouse, with the Micawbers ; but Mr. Micawber, meeting him again after a lapse of years, can drink " to the days when my friend Copperfield and myself were younger, and fought our way in the world side by side." On their first meeting again, at Canterbury, when David tells him that he is now at school, he can remark : " Although a mind like my friend Copperfield's does not require that cultivation which, without his knowledge of men and things, it would require, still it is a rich soil teeming with latent vegetation." Later, when they meet in the company of Traddles, Mr. Micawber refers to his affairs as a somewhat romantic historian, engaged in the chronicle of the whole world, might refer to the position of some great empire at a crisis in its history :

"You find us, Copperfield," said Mr. Micawber, with one eye on Traddles, "at present established, on what may be designated as a small and unassuming scale ; but, you are aware that I have, in the course of my career, surmounted difficulties, and conquered obstacles. You are no stranger to the fact, that there have been periods of my life, when it has been requisite that I should pause, until certain unexpected events should turn up ; when it has been necessary that I should fall back, before making what I trust I shall not be accused of presumption in terming—a spring. The present is one of those momentous stages in the life of man. You find me, fallen back, *for* a spring ; and I have every reason to believe that a vigorous leap will shortly be the result."

And his subsequent review of the situation, his parting speech, in the manner in which it succeeds in casting a curious glamour over everything, transforming the most trumpery and prosaic matter into something rich and strange, gives us the complete Micawber, soaring high above this world of " offices and the witness-box " :

"My dear Copperfield, I need hardly tell you that to have beneath our roof, under existing circumstances, a mind like that which gleams—if I may be allowed the expression—which gleams—in your friend Traddles, is an unspeakable comfort. With a washerwoman, who exposes hard-bake for sale in her parlor-window, dwelling next door, and a Bow-street officer residing over the way, you may imagine that his society is a source of consolation to myself and to Mrs. Micawber. I am at present, my dear Copperfield, engaged in the sale of corn upon commission. It is not an avocation of a remunerative description—in other words, it does *not* pay—and some temporary embarrassments of a pecuniary nature have been the consequence. I am, however, delighted to add that I have now an immediate prospect of something turning up (I am not at liberty to say in what direction), which I trust will enable me to provide, permanently, both for myself and for your friend Traddles, in whom I have an unaffected interest. You may, perhaps, be prepared to hear that Mrs. Micawber is in a state of health which renders it not wholly improbable that an addition may be ultimately made to those pledges of affection which —in short, to the infantine group. Mrs. Micawber's family have been so good as to express their dissatisfaction at this state of things. I have merely to observe that I am not aware it is any business of theirs, and that I repel that exhibition of feeling with scorn, and with defiance ! "

An excellent example of our friend's Front Bench manner, in which every polysyllabic phrase suggests at least five thousand a year and a substantial pension. What is an empty pocket compared to such verbal riches ? Selling corn upon commission may be a poor business, but once it is referred to as " not an avocation of a remunerative description " it somehow suggests that immense wealth is lying only just beyond the speaker's grasp ; it takes us immediately into an atmosphere of prosperity. What is a balance at the bank to a man who has only to open his mouth to shower riches about him like some one in a fairy tale, whose very tongue is an alchemist ?

Living in the world as he does, not as some poor devil trying to patch together a bare existence and evade his creditors, but as the central and heroic figure in that amazing chronicle, The Life and Times of Wilkins Micawber, Lover, Husband, Father, Financier, and Philosopher, Mr. Micawber instinctively seizes hold of every situation, good or evil, that presents itself and makes the most of it. Faced with such romantic gusto, so fine an appreciation of a crisis, revelling even in profound despair and last farewells, ill fortune, try as it may, can hardly make itself felt. And the commonplace, that drab stuff which is the fabric of most of our days, vanishes entirely : it is hardly conceivable that Mr. Micawber can ever have had a dull moment. It would be difficult to imagine anything more dreary than the prospect of being a clerk to a petty solicitor in a small cathedral town, or anything less exciting and romantic than a family removal from London to Canterbury ; but Mr. Micawber, on the eve of his removal to Uriah Heep's, stands before us as a man who has just seen Troy burn and is now about to embark on an Odyssey. And so, of course, he is : it is we who are blind and deaf and spirit-less in our boredom. " It may be expected," the great creature declares to his friends, " that on the eve of a migration which will consign us to a perfectly new existence, I should offer a few valedictory remarks to two such friends as I see before me. But all that I have to say in this way, I have said. Whatever station in society I may attain, through the medium of the learned profession of which I am about to become an unworthy member, I shall endeavour not to disgrace, and Mrs. Micawber will be safe to adorn." Being able now to cast off his disguise (the name " Mortimer " and a pair of spectacles—and who can doubt that he enjoyed both immensely ?), he speaks as one who has long been an exile or spent half a lifetime in remote hiding-places, and his language leaps up to grapple with the romantic moment : " The cloud has passed from the dreary scene, and the God of Day is once more high upon the mountain tops. On Monday next, on the arrival of the four o'clock afternoon coach at Canterbury, my foot will be on my native heath—my name, Micawber."

No sooner is Australia mentioned (" the land, the only land, for myself and my family "—though he has ob-viously never given it a thought before) than he sees a new part for himself and plunges into it. Within an hour or so, we are told, he is walking the streets of

Canterbury—" expressing, in the hardy roving manner he assumed, the unsettled habits of a temporary sojourner in the land ; and looking at the bullocks, as they came by, with the eye of an Australian farmer." And as the plans for emigration mature, he becomes still more wildly colonial. What could be better than the steps he has taken to familiarise himself and his family with the conditions of Australian life ?

" My eldest daughter attends at five every morning at a neighbouring establishment, to acquire the process —if process it may be called—of milking cows. My younger children are instructed to observe, as closely as circumstances will permit, the habits of the pigs and poultry maintained in the poorer parts of this city : a pursuit from which they have, on two occasions, been brought home, within an inch of being run over. I have myself directed some attention, during the past week, to the art of baking ; and my son Wilkins has issued forth with a walking-stick and driven cattle, when permitted, by the rugged hirelings who had them in charge, to render any voluntary service in that direction—which I regret to say, for the credit of our nature, was not often ; he being generally warned, with imprecations, to desist."

Once on board the ship, he combines, with great skill, both the colonial and nautical characters. With a low-crowned straw hat, a complete suit of oilskins, a telescope, and a trick of " casting up his eye at the sky as looking out for dirty weather," he is nothing less than an old salt,

and we can be sure that he carried out his intention of
spinning an occasional yarn before the galley-fire.   And
he has also provided himself and his family with enormous
clasp-knives and wooden spoons, and insists upon their
drinking out of "villainous little tin pots" although
there are plenty of glasses in the room, so determined is
he that they shall stand before Albion as "denizens of
the forest." "The luxuries of the old country we
abandon," he announces with an intense pleasure that is
the very height of luxury.   Happy Mr. Micawber, with
every hour adding pages to his romantic history, moving
sublimely in a world of his own creation, clad in the armour
of his soaring fancy, the conqueror of circumstance,
merely adding its variations to his swelling moods as he
adds the lemons to the punch.   He is a greater figure in
the history of romantic idealism than most of its professors,
for he lays bare more of its secrets, as he rolls out his
"few remarks" and points his single eyeglass over the
steaming bowl, than whole volumes of our Schellings
and Schlegels.   Happy Mr. Micawber, joyously com-
bining the rôles of financier, sailor, and pioneer, but, in
truth, only travelling in a dream, from an England that
was never there to an Australia that he will invent,
sailing from moonshine to moonshine.

It was a fortunate day for Mr. Micawber when he
visited a certain house (presumably in Plymouth) and

heard the daughter of the family sing her two ballads, *The Dashing White Serjeant* and *Little Tafflin*, for by the time he had heard *Little Tafflin*, we are told, he had resolved to win the fair singer or perish in the attempt, and, as we know, was successful, so that Emma became in due course the companion of his travels, his partner in joy and sorrow, Mrs. Micawber. He could not have made a better choice. Mrs. Micawber is entitled to a place, by the side of Lady Macbeth, among the great wives of literature. Micawber himself is a great man, but we must not allow our appreciation of that fact to blind us to another fact, namely, that great as he is, he would be like a ship robbed of its compass without " that pervading influence which sanctifies while it enhances the—in short, the influence of Woman in the lofty character of Wife." There never was a man more suitably and happily mated. If an unswerving loyalty, an unconquerable fidelity, are necessary to the character of a good wife, as they are, then Mrs. Micawber takes her place among the best, for her loyalty and fidelity are almost matchless. Though buffeted by the world, pursued by duns, hampered by her ever-increasing family, at odds with her relatives, she will never desert Mr. Micawber. If there should be any cynic who should doubt the strength of her attachment, let him read once more the chronicles of the Micawbers, and he will be

compelled to agree : Mrs. Micawber will never desert
Mr. Micawber. If a certain similarity in tastes and
temperament is one of the conditions of a happy marriage, as it is, this similarity is not difficult to find in the
Micawbers. Fortunately, Mrs. Micawber has all her
husband's elasticity, his power of rising from the depths
of despair to the heights of conviviality in an incredibly
short space of time. Had she been a woman of another
temperament, a creature of fixed moods, gazing with
stony eyes at the rapidly oscillating needle of her husband's
humour, all her loyalty would have been to little purpose :
the God of Day would inevitably have gone down upon
the dreary scene. But she is as elastic as he is. " I have
known her," David tells us, " to be thrown into fainting
fits by the king's taxes at three o'clock, and to eat lamb-
chops breaded, and drink warm ale (paid for with two
teaspoons that had gone to the pawnbroker's), at four.
On one occasion, when an execution had just been put
in, coming home through some chance as early as six
o'clock, I saw her lying (of course with a twin) under
the grate in a swoon, with her hair all torn about her
face ; but I never knew her more cheerful than she was,
that very same night, over a veal-cutlet before the
kitchen fire, telling me stories about her papa and mamma,
and the company they used to keep." But a happy
marriage demands not only unity but variety. The two

partners must not be identical in character, a mere reflection of one another, but must be sufficiently diverse so that each one can put something into the joint concern that the other partner lacks, so that they can act as both a check and a stimulus upon one another. Does this final condition clang the gates before Mrs. Micawber's face, barring her out of the ultimate Eden ? It does not.

If Wilkins is the imaginative partner, the rhetorician, of the Micawbers, Emma is the logician. Her task it is to stand behind her fiery and impetuous spouse, restraining him until she has pointed the way. Never was a devoted woman better equipped for the task. " Emma's form is fragile, but her grasp of a subject is inferior to none," her father was in the habit of saying, and undoubtedly her father was a man of some discernment. Mrs. Micawber's grasp of a subject compels our admiration. Mr. Micawber, with his swelling and opulent imagination, is capable of conceiving the most colossal projects and of hurling himself into the fray, but to Mrs. Micawber is left the arduous task of clearing away, with a ruthlessness that appals lesser intellects, the non-essentials of a problem and then of stating it, in its barest terms, with an exquisite and almost superhuman lucidity. Not even in the early days of Political Economy, the days of the Economic Man, when the textbooks were as repulsive as they are to-day but differed from our modern works in being intelligible, were economic problems stated so clearly as they are by Mrs. Micawber. Her approach to the matter of the Medway Coal Trade is a model of reasoning :

"We all came back again," replied Mrs. Micawber. "Since then, I have consulted other branches of my family on the course which it is most expedient for Mr. Micawber to take—for I maintain that he must take some course, Master Copperfield," said Mrs. Micawber, argumentatively. "It is clear that a family of six, not including a domestic, cannot live upon air."

"Certainly, ma'am," said I.

"The opinion of those other branches of my family," pursued Mrs. Micawber, "is, that Mr. Micawber should immediately turn his attention to coals."

"To what, ma'am ? "

"To coals," said Mrs. Micawber. "To the coal trade. Mr. Micawber was induced to think, on inquiry, that there might be an opening for a man of his talent in the Medway Coal Trade. Then, as Mr. Micawber very properly said, the first step to be taken clearly was, to come and *see* the Medway. Which we came and saw. I say 'we,' Master Copperfield ; for I never will," said Mrs. Micawber with emotion, "I never will desert Mr. Micawber."

I murmured my admiration and approbation.

"We came," repeated Mrs. Micawber, "and saw the Medway. My opinion of the coal trade on that river, is, that it may require talent, but that it certainly requires capital. Talent, Mr. Micawber has ; capital, Mr. Micawber has not. We saw, I think, the greater

part of the Medway; and that is my individual conclusion. Being so near here, Mr. Micawber was of
opinion that it would be rash not to come on, and see
the Cathedral. Firstly, on account of its being so well
worth seeing, and our never having seen it; and secondly,
on account of the great probability of something turning
up in a cathedral town. . . ."

Apart from that one emotional outburst on this subject
of never deserting Mr. Micawber, not only excusable
but even admirable in itself, showing as it does that the
crystal-clear brain is only the servant of a woman's warm
heart, a treatise by a master of the subject could not achieve
greater lucidity. Equally good is her later survey, at
the dinner-party given by David, when she goes into the
whole question of her husband's prospects with characteristic thoroughness and grasp. Coals are not to be
relied upon; and corn, we are told, though gentlemanly
is not remunerative—" Commission to the extent of two
and ninepence in a fortnight cannot, however limited
our ideas, be considered remunerative." Brewing and
banking are both discussed by this devoted and clear-
sighted helpmate, but both have shown themselves
adamant in the face of Mr. Micawber's offers. It is
clear, as Mrs. Micawber remarks, that we must live.
What is to be done? Let us hear the lady herself on
the subject, and so discover her at the height of her
powers :

" Very well," said Mrs. Micawber.   " Then what do
I recommend ?   Here is Mr. Micawber with a variety
of qualifications—with great talent——"

" Really, my love," said Mr. Micawber.

" Pray, my dear, allow me to conclude.   Here is
Mr. Micawber, with a variety of qualifications, with
great talent—I should say, with genius, but that may be
the partiality of a wife——"

Traddles and I both murmured " No."

" And here is Mr. Micawber without any suitable
position or employment.   Where does that responsibility
rest ?   Clearly on society.   Then I would make a fact
so disgraceful known, and boldly challenge society to
set it right.   It appears to me, my dear Mr. Copperfield,"
said Mrs. Micawber, forcibly, " that what Mr. Micawber
has to do, is to throw down the gauntlet to society, and
say, in effect, ' Show me who will take that up.   Let
the party immediately step forward.' "

I ventured to ask Mrs. Micawber how this was to
be done.

" By advertising," said Mrs. Micawber—" in all the
papers.   It appears to me, that what Mr. Micawber has
to do, in justice to himself, in justice to his family, and
I will even go so far as to say in justice to society, by which
he has been hitherto overlooked, is to advertise in all the
papers ;   to describe himself plainly as so-and-so, with
such and such qualifications, and to put it thus : ' *Now*
employ me, on remunerative terms, and address, post-
paid, to *W. M.*, Post Office, Camden Town.' "

Does Mr. Micawber think of taking up the Law—then
Mrs. Micawber is quick to ask whether, in applying

himself to a subordinate branch of the profession, he will place it out of his power to rise ultimately to the " top of the tree," seeing him, in her mind's eye, as a Judge or a Chancellor.   When Australia is suggested, she is on hand to inquire as to the climate and the circumstances of the country—are they such that a man of Mr. Micawber's abilities would have a fair chance of rising in the social scale ?   When they are actually on the boat, how nobly she devotes herself to the task of making her husband (who has declared that " Britannia must take her chance ") see that his duty, in this distant clime, will be to strengthen and not to weaken the connection between himself and Albion.   No wife could do more in furthering the best interests of her husband and of society at one and the same time.   How inspiring is her very last piece of advice :

" I wish Mr. Micawber to take his stand upon that vessel's prow, and firmly say, ' This country I am come to conquer !   Have you honours ?   Have you riches ? Have you posts of profitable pecuniary emolument ? Let them be brought forward.   They are mine.' "

Mr. Micawber, glancing at us all, seemed to think there was a good deal in this idea.

" I wish Mr. Micawber, if I make myself understood," said Mrs. Micawber, in her argumentative tone, " to be the Caesar of his own fortunes.   That, my dear Mr. Copperfield, appears to be his true position.   From the first moment of this voyage, I wish Mr. Micawber to

stand upon that vessel's prow and say, ' Enough of delay :
enough of disappointment : enough of limited means.
That was in the old country.   This is the new   Produce
your reparation.   Bring it forward ! ' "

After this, there is no excuse for Mr. Micawber if he
does not " wield the rod of talent and of power in Australia."   A fine fighting spirit, womanly wit, and a
devoted heart can do no more for him.

Mrs. Micawber is one of the severest logicians with
whom we have ever been acquainted ; but she is not
really reasoning about this world at all : she lives in
Mr. Micawber's world, and, indeed, represents the logical
and scientific point of view in that world.   Existing as
she does in the fire and light of Mr Micawber's rich
imagination, walking for ever in his gigantic shadow, it
naturally follows that she has long since lost sight of
common reality, which has been swallowed up by the
strange and romantic world created for himself by
Mr. Micawber.   And since there is no reason why such
a world, however strange and romantic and shadowy
it may be, should not have its own logicians, we find
Mrs. Micawber in the part, thereby supplementing her
husband's more emotional, rhetorical, and imaginative
outlook, manner, and speech, completing—as it were—
his world for him just as she rounds off his life by her
partnership in their happy marriage.   Nor is it strange

that a lady who, notwithstanding her fragility of form, has a grasp of a subject inferior to none, should be so consistently and happily moonstruck. The rich and fiery imagination, incessantly creating, must always acquire the ascendancy : the most austere and determined logic can never, in the last resort, be anything more than its willing servant. Ourselves both creations and creative, living half in and half out of some gigantic tragi-comedy of black night and unnumbered stars, in which we willy-nilly play a part laid down for us and yet contrive before we have done to have some tiny say in its authorship, putting in a cry here, a gesture there, that are our own, we must instinctively recognise and do homage to the creative imagination, bearing as it does the marks of divinity, so that sooner or later we come under its spell and are wetted by its spectral rain and warmed by its fabulous suns. In the fable, perhaps the loveliest and most significant of them all, of the crazy knight, Sancho Panza is most grossly and realistically minded, a man of common-sense, with his eyes fixed on solid objects ; and yet after he has jogged behind his master down so many winding roads, he becomes in the end as high fantastical as the Don himself and capers among enchantments. So too Mrs. Micawber, for all her fierce feminine lucidity, has taken to her bosom not only the person of Mr. Micawber but all his host of dreams and legends, so that she too moves happily among enchantments, the picture of a good wife and a fitting subject for innumerable parables.

Nothing has been said so far about the part that Mr. Micawber is made to play in the story, a part that has been severely criticised, not least by his greatest admirers. Of the emigration and Mr. Micawber's purely material success at the end of the story, Mr. Chesterton has remarked : "But how did it happen that the man who created this Micawber could pension him off at the end of the story and make him a successful colonial mayor ? Micawber never did succeed, never ought to succeed ; his kingdom is not of this world." This is well said ; but even if we agree with this view of Micawber, it is possible to defend Dickens. If the material success is offered us as a kind of poetic justice (and the choice of the Colonies suggests this, as the Victorians seemed to regard the Colonies as a rough-and-ready kind of Christian Heaven, with a scheme of poetic justice that would reward, let us say, the Squire's son, who has been wrongly accused of forgery and promptly exiled, with ten thousand head of sheep), then it is entirely unnecessary, for Mr. Micawber himself is a kind of poet, who lives in poetry, and does not need poetic justice. But if it is simply regarded as a new setting for Mr. Micawber, giving him, as it were, more scope for his Micawberishness, then it can be justified. Our last news of him is as "a diligent and esteemed correspondent" of the *Port Middlebay Times*, and obviously he was entirely at ease, as happy as a king, dashing off leaders for that influential organ. Is there anything nearer Micawber in this world than the early Colonial and American Press, existing sumptuously on magnificent phrases, rhetoric, and capital letters? Once the actual work had begun and the pioneers were busy, Micawber was worth his weight in diamonds and rubies to any colony (not merely as a character—as that, he was worth his weight anywhere) as a rhetorician, a fount of glorious phrases, an ever-gushing spring of eloquence, as the very embodiment of the romantic outlook upon life, of unconquerable faith and hope. Hard labour and easy rhetoric have tamed many a wilderness. Pioneering demands, first, the great workers, and then, afterwards, the great talkers; and it is not merely a coincidence that of all modern states America should have produced the largest crop of orators and offered them the greatest rewards. Mr. Micawber, I have no doubt, talked Port Middlebay into existence, and so deserved its highest honours.

But of his part as a detective in the history of David Copperfield it is impossible to put forward any defence. It is impossible to read those chapters without feeling that Micawber is being constrained by his creator: even the humour is forced and unreal. Indeed, the whole episode is preposterous. Uriah Heep would never have dreamed of employing such a person ; Mr. Micawber would never have remained in the office a week ; and, even supposing that both actions were possible, he would never have been able to conceal his knowledge of Uriah's shady transactions or, what is yet more unlikely, have been able to ferret them all out, tabulate them in a formal document, and then bide his time until the proper moment for disclosure had arrived. Mr. Micawber as a financial detective is no more convincing than Shelley as a Bow Street runner. This trick of hurling his great drolls into the plot of the story and compelling them to play some quite unlikely part is, of course, one of the most notable defects in Dickens. Nor can we understand how a man could have the wit to create such creatures and yet the folly to treat them so badly, until we reflect that we do not regard a Dickens tale as he regarded it. We think the stories exist for the sake of the characters ; we do not care what happens so long as the delicious creatures make their appearance from time to time ; many of us, who know the Dickens characters as we know our friends, could not set down on paper a single plot of his, having long since forgotten the machinery of the tale. But Dickens, an extremely conscientious author, thought that the characters existed for the sake of the stories—it is only in *Pickwick* that the characters exist for their own sweet sakes ; and so when he had created some colossal droll, a Micawber, a Pecksniff, a Skimpole, and the like, he felt that he had to justify the space taken up by the great creature and so forced him to further the interests of the plot, usually in some outrageous manner. This was only the view of the conventional author, the superficial Dickens ; the real man knew better and, in his heart of hearts, realised that these great comic figures of his were their own excuse and needed no complicated intrigue to justify their existence. Had he not realised this, he would never have allowed them to occupy so much room in his story, but would have curtailed their antics and bound them fast to the plot.

There is only one thing better than a story, and that is—a character. A character is half-a-hundred stories at once, the source of endless fables ; and it is something more, particularly if it is a comic character. The tragic figures can hardly be separated from their particular chronicles, for we envisage them in the awful light of their destiny and doom ; but the great comic figures wander out of their books, which are only so many introductions to them, for they are nothing if not children of freedom, and so we find them and their starry folly at large in our minds. The books themselves we may have forgotten, their very names may have faded out of our memories, but these figures, long since our friends that we are ready to laugh and cry over, we do not forget. Their happy absurdities have added something to the whole flavour of our existence : these great fools, dissolving us into laughter, have touched our minds with the mellow philosophy of their creators : leaving their company, the parlour door closed behind us, the tavern lights that illumined them now blurred in the wind and rain, we question the night, which has swallowed our last peal of laughter, more curiously, and await, in a heightened mood of expectancy, the pageant and comedy of the approaching day. Only this humour of character can stir the depths. The humour of incident and situation that does not proceed from character, however artfully it may be contrived, is at its best only an elaborate play, making a glitter and commotion on the surface of things. But the humour of character goes down and touches, surely but tenderly, the very roots of our common human nature.

BY THE SAME AUTHOR

FIGURES IN MODERN LITERATURE

Second Edition. Demy 8vo. 7s. 6d. net.

" Mr. Priestley succeeds, with a delightful appearance of ease, in providing good prose, good criticism, and good fun at one and the same time. The result is the best first book of its kind that has appeared for many years, a book that is quite evidently the work of one of the finest critical minds of this generation. Of the nine authors dealt with, seven—all important writers—have never been treated at any length before : Mr. Squire, Mr. Santayana, Mr. Saintsbury, Mr. Lynd, Mr. Jacobs, Mr. A. E. Housman, and the late Maurice Hewlett. Of the two remaining essays—on Mr. de la Mare and on Mr. Arnold Bennett—it is sufficient to say that they are beyond comparison the best things that have been written on their respective subjects. Indeed, the study of Mr. de la Mare is a masterpiece of criticism."—*Daily News*.

" Mr. Priestley has such an air of persuasion, of conviction and reasonableness, in writing of his contemporaries, that the reader is immediately at ease; he feels that he is in the company of a guide who is kindly and acute, learned and not capricious. He never fails to interest you vividly in his analysis, for he has a fine fluent style in which the wit is woven to its purpose."—*Saturday Review*.

" His judgments are exquisitely poised. There is not one eccentric piece of general critical meditation in the whole book, or one dull one. And its sidelights on the mechanism of writing—those on the function of style, for instance, and on punctuation — are as valuable as they are unaffected."—*Punch*.

JOHN LANE THE BODLEY HEAD LTD., VIGO STREET, W.1

I FOR ONE

Crown 8vo.   6s. net.

" Mr. Priestley has the real stuff of an essayist in him. He reveals a personality—and a charming one—as every essayist worth his salt must do. It is a personality full of human sympathies, with a ripe but not boisterous humour. He proves his descent from the great lineage of essayists."
Times Literary Supplement.

" Mr. Priestley has done it again.   Already recognised by the discriminating as one of the best of our younger essayists, he now fulfils the promise and repeats the achievement of his ' Papers from Liliput.' His prose achieves that air of spontaneity which is the last reward of the careful stylist ; it has the confidence and ease of familiar talk."—*Spectator*.

"His prose is virile, sensitive, beautifully phrased, and seldom or never strained. ' This Insubstantial Pageant' and ' In the Country' are essays written in a prose as beautiful as any I remember these many years. If a novel appeared to-morrow containing Mr. Priestley's wit and skill, it would be the most talked-of book of the year. ' I for One' is wholly delightful."—*Daily News*.

" Mr. Priestley has the qualifications of the born essayist. He has the noticing eye and the candid mind of humour, whether he looks at and considers himself or other people ; he has the keen interest in mundane affairs that perceives ' comedies and tragedies ripening under every chimney-pot' ; and he has, most important qualification of all, perhaps, since it is the one which distinguishes, or at any rate which would in a perfect world distinguish, the writer from the mere intelligent human being, the power of using naturally the amassed riches of language."—*Time and Tide*.

JOHN LANE THE BODLEY HEAD LTD., VIGO STREET, W.1

THE WEEK-END LIBRARY

A new series of reprints of books of established reputation attractively produced in uniform style and in
a size suitable for reading on a journey or in bed.

Foolscap 8vo.   3s. 6d. net each volume.

FIRST VOLUMES

THE TWILIGHT OF THE GODS. By RICHARD
  GARNETT.   With an Introduction by T. E.
  LAWRENCE.

ORTHODOXY. By G. K. CHESTERTON.

SCHOLAR-GIPSIES. By JOHN BUCHAN.

SELECTED STORIES OF ANATOLE FRANCE.
  Arranged, with a Foreword, by J. LEWIS MAY.

SOME REMINISCENCES OF A NEW GUINEA
  RESIDENT MAGISTRATE: First Series.   By
  CAPTAIN C. A. W. MONCKTON.

SOME REMINISCENCES OF A NEW GUINEA
  RESIDENT MAGISTRATE: Second Series.   By
  CAPTAIN C. A. W. MONCKTON.

WITH SILENT FRIENDS. By RICHARD KING.

THE HANDLING OF WORDS. By VERNON LEE.

HORTUS VITAE: Essays on the Gardening of Life.
  By VERNON LEE.

UNADDRESSED LETTERS.   By SIR FRANK
  SWETTENHAM.

Other volumes in preparation

JOHN LANE THE BODLEY HEAD LTD., VIGO STREET, W.1

THE WEEK-END LIBRARY

A new series of reprints of books of established reputation attractively produced in uniform style and in a size suitable for reading on a journey or in bed.

Foolscap 8vo.   3s. 6d. net each volume.

First Volumes

CANADIAN WONDER TALES.   By Cyrus Macmillan.   With a Foreword by Sir George Peterson.

BEHIND THE BEYOND.   By Stephen Leacock.

THE FUGGER NEWS-LETTERS: First Series. Edited by Victor von Klarwill.   Translated by Pauline de Chary.   With a Foreword by H. Gordon Selfridge.

THE GOOD SOLDIER.   By Ford Madox Ford.

HERETICS.   By G. K. Chesterton.

THE ENGLISH COMIC CHARACTERS.   By J. B. Priestley.

INTERLUDES AND POEMS.   By Lascelles Abercrombie.

THE ROMANCE OF EXCAVATION.   By David Masters.

THE NAPOLEON OF NOTTING HILL.   By G. K. Chesterton.

Other volumes in preparation

JOHN LANE THE BODLEY HEAD LTD., VIGO STREET, W.1

THE NOVELS OF BENJAMIN DISRAELI EARL OF BEACONSFIELD

A new uniform thin paper edition.

Foolscap 8vo.   3s. 6d. net each volume.

JOHN LANE THE BODLEY HEAD LTD., VIGO STREET, W.1

THE WORKS OF
ANATOLE FRANCE
IN ENGLISH

Edited by the late Frederic Chapman
and J. Lewis May

THE LIBRARY EDITION

Demy 8vo, in uniform binding, with
end-papers by Aubrey Beardsley

7s. 6d. net each volume.

THE NEW POPULAR EDITION

Cloth.   Crown 8vo.   2s. 6d. net each volume.

Leather.   Crown 8vo.   5s. net each volume.

" Messrs. John Lane are making it uncommonly difficult
for any one to put up a defence who has not read some at
least of the works produced by the rich genius of Anatole
France.   The Popular Edition, with its good clear printing,
is a most attractive bargain in these desperate times."
Manchester Guardian.

" Admirers of Anatole France—and the list is legion—
owe a good deal to Messrs. John Lane for their New Popular
Edition."—*Sunday Times.*

JOHN LANE THE BODLEY HEAD LTD., VIGO STREET, W.1

THE GOLDEN HIND SERIES

A new uniform series of biographies of the great explorers, published under the general editorship of MILTON WALDMAN.

Illustrated. Demy 8vo. 12s. 6d. net each volume.

FIRST VOLUMES

SIR FRANCIS DRAKE
By E. F. BENSON.

CAPTAIN JOHN SMITH
By E. KEBLE CHATTERTON.

HENRY HUDSON
By LLEWELYN POWYS.

SIR WALTER RALEIGH
By MILTON WALDMAN.

SIR JOHN HAWKINS
By PHILIP GOSSE.

SIR MARTIN FROBISHER
By WILLIAM McFEE.

SIR RICHARD GRENVILLE
By J. C. SQUIRE.

WILLIAM DAMPIER
By CLENNELL WILKINSON.

Other volumes in preparation

JOHN LANE THE BODLEY HEAD LTD., VIGO STREET, W.1